The Heart  of a Mother

Kathleen Nelson

BtoZ Publishing
El Paso, Texas

The Heart of a Mother
by Kathleen Nelson

Copyright 2011, by Kathleen Nelson
725 Montclair Dr.
El Paso, TX 79932
www.btozpublishing.com
www.premeditatedparenting.net

All Scripture quotations, unless otherwise indicated are from the
Holy Bible, New International Version © 1973, 1978, 1984
by International Bible Society. Used by permission
of Zondervan Bible Publishers. All rights reserved.

Scripture quotations marked (NASB) are from the *New American Standard Bible.*
© 1960, 1962, 1963, 1968, 1971, 1972, 1973, 1975, 1977, 1995 by The Lockman
Foundation. All rights reserved.

Scripture quotations marked (NCV) are from the *New Century Version.* © 1987, 1988, 1991 by Word Publishing. All rights reserved.

Cover design: Blaise and Silas Nelson
Editor: Blaise Nelson

The Potter's Masterpiece on the front cover is by Perry Horner.
Copyright owned by New Hope Pregnancy Care Center.
Used by permission. All rights reserved.
For more information on *The Potter's Masterpiece* please visit:
New Hope Pregnancy Care Center at P.O. Box 5183, Cleveland, TN 37320-5183,
www.newhopepcc.org, (423) 479-5825.

Published by BtoZ Publishing
El Paso, Texas

ISBN # 978-1467979641

Table of Contents

Prologue 5

Introduction 13

Positioning Yourself 19

Neediness 21

It's Spiritual Work 23

Establishing Your Vision 29

A Season 29

God's Gift 37

Missing the True Value 43

Shaping a Life 46

The Exchange of Lives 53

Your Calling 59

Rebuilding Your Identity 67

A Puzzle 71

Starting Over 73

Expired Dreams 76

The Call of Every Believer 80

God Called You 85

A Life Coach 89

A Discipler 92

A Drip Line 93

Infinite Impact 94

Investment 98

My Little Box 101

Reinforcing Your Perseverance 103

Discerning Voices 104

Resisting Idols 105

Go to God 110

The Truth Project 113

A Storehouse 116

Focus 117

Eliminate 121

Boundaries 124

Do the Next Right Thing 127

A Mother in Progress 128

An Imperfect Mother 134

Conclusion 139

Appendix 143

Verse Index 145

Index 147

Discussion Questions 151

Prologue

In the fall of 1990, I married my sweetheart, Steve. Three years later, Blaise Lewis Nelson was born. On the night he was born, the world stood still for both Steve and me. We had no idea that having our own son was going to be that wonderful and have such a profound effect on us. There are no words to describe how much we loved and adored our new son.

Yet just as our son was introduced into the world that night, a very long and intense internal struggle was introduced to my soul. God was calling me to yield in a way that I had never experienced before. Somehow, I sensed that God wanted me to relinquish my life and raise this child for Him. Up until that point in my life, I had never truly sacrificed so much for anyone before.

I clearly remember when I finally broke and completely yielded to what God was calling me to be in my motherhood. I was eight months pregnant with my second baby, and Steve had just become a pastor in our local church. We attended a National Pastors' Conference in Missouri. One of the older, godly mothers at the conference spoke about motherhood. Although I was trying to take notes and pay attention to every word she said, I was weeping through the whole talk. Because I was blowing my nose and wiping my eyes the entire time, I didn't even hear very much of her seminar. But I did hear God – very clearly. God was doing an amazing work in my heart. He was calling me, and I was hearing Him. Everything in my soul was saying, "Yes, God, I want to yield. I want to lay down my life for these little souls that You have entrusted to me. I want to be the all-in, no-holds-barred, pour-out-my-life-for-my-children type of mother!"

To be completely honest, I never was the same after that. God got a hold of me. Interestingly, during those first two years as a mother, I repeatedly prayed that God would develop in me a heart and a passion for motherhood. He answered that prayer in ways that I never could have imagined.

Jump ahead a few years to late spring of 2002. At the time, I was the proud mother of five little ones, with the oldest being eight years old. That summer, several young moms in my church wanted to get together weekly. They asked me to encourage them in their motherhood. Because I was in a very busy phase of life, I wasn't sure it was going to be possible for me to commit to these weekly meetings.

After Steve and I discussed it, he thought it sounded like a good idea despite my busy schedule. We decided that I would go down to the local Bible store and pick out some materials to lead the women through a motherhood Bible study. I came home and told Steve that I wasn't peaceful with using any of the books I found. I explained that I felt like God had given me something different to share—something not found in those books in the store. Steve suggested that I take some time that upcoming summer to write out exactly what God taught me, so that I could share it with that group of mothers.

That summer the Lord poured out His Spirit and led me as I developed the "Motherhood Conference." Miraculously, I was able to thoroughly record everything that the Lord had taught me so far as I had walked through my motherhood. I remember as I was writing that summer, I sensed an incredible, supernatural power at work in me. Even though I was in such a hectic, demanding phase of raising the children, I truly sensed that God was spiritually intervening in the development of those teaching materials. I definitely felt like I was playing the part of the clay, not the potter.

Weeks later, I shared that material with ten mothers in my living room. Soon after that, another request came for me to share my journey with another group of mothers, again in someone's living room. Then there was another request. The meetings slowly started involving larger groups of mothers. Eventually, God guided us to present the Bible study materials in a conference setting. Gradually, God began to export the Bible study outside of our little local venues. Since those early days, I have flown to different cities around the country to share with mothers. God seems to stir mothers during those times, and women often tell me that they have been challenged and encouraged in their mothering. I have had the opportunity to share the Motherhood Conference eleven times over the last several years. I constantly see the need for it.

Every time I go to the store, I stage silent conversations in my head with young moms who are struggling with their children. I imagine myself boldly walking up to them and offering them some helpful advice. Sometimes I pretend my words are encouraging. Sometimes I imagine my words to be challenging.

I recently tried it when I was shopping at Office Depot. I gently approached a young mother whose child was screaming bloody murder and throwing a royal hissy-fit. I warmly invited her to a parenting class that we were having at our church. It didn't go so well. She quickly became offended and resentfully told me that she was a public school teacher and she didn't need any parenting classes. Unbeknownst to me, her husband had come around the corner behind me as this scene was playing out. As she filled him in on what was happening, I lightly jogged – okay, I literally ran! – out of the store. I jumped into my inconspicuous fifteen-passenger van, and peeled out. I've never quite had the courage to try that again. I'm still recovering from how badly that attempt went!

As the years pass, my desire to encourage and challenge Christian mothers has only intensified. From that first time as a young mom at the conference in Missouri to the present, God has kept that passion burning. God has taught me so much along the way. He continues to stir me in my zeal for motherhood. Mothering is my heartbeat. Furthermore, I am fully convinced that my heart for mothering is a gift from God. What He has done in my heart and family has truly been Him and His Spirit, far more than my vision or determination. I have been the *recipient* of this passion, not the originator or author.

I write to you with a multi-faceted agenda. First, I pray that God will, in some way, use this book in your life, your home, and with your children. I write to you with the hope that God will also awaken you and draw you to Himself. I pray that He gives you your own God-originated, burning passion for motherhood.

I also write this book with a bigger, farther-reaching dream. My heart is that God will regain His rightful glory that we Christians forfeit as we fall prey to the world's lies and allurements. When the lost world looks at the Christian family, they should see something special. Shouldn't it be that the lost would actually desire Christ because of what they see in our homes and lives? Shouldn't it be that, as the world watches God's people, they undeniably witness the blessing of God for those who seek and follow Him?

Frankly, God's people are not the role models of parents in this world. They should be, but they are not. It's a sad commentary on the state of Christianity that we often turn to the world for parenting ideas, lacking the confidence to cling to God. We Christians have not followed the Lord closely or reverently enough for us to stake His flag on the battlefield of parenting! This has everything to do with our disobedience, and nothing to do with God's trustworthiness!

I've visited with Christian mothers who ask me what I think of one parenting idea or another. I sometimes ask them where they get these ideas. They often name a magazine or TV show and confess that the ideas are from a godless source. I appreciate that moms are desperate for any advice they can get, but God's ways have to be our anchor.

I specifically remember speaking with one mother. Vulnerably, she told me how she had been struggling to understand her daughter for years. As we visited, this mother told me she had found a new book that clearly revealed to her what she had been wrestling with about her girl. I asked her who the author was and what his credentials were. My Christian friend confessed that the author was not a believer; he was a renowned child psychologist. It was difficult to listen to her because she was genuinely relieved and comforted by her new findings. Yet, in my spirit, I knew that God wanted me to direct her back to Him.

As she explained her new theory about her daughter, I tried to graciously ask her how that theory lined up with Scripture. I specifically remember asking her if she could think of one verse that aligned to the theories presented in her new book. Understandably, she was somewhat flabbergasted by my questioning; however, that conversation actually ended well. I think she understood my hesitancy with her newfound theories. Shouldn't we love one another enough to do that for each other? If I am adopting worldly ideas and principles, I would only hope that a fellow believer would love me enough to point me back to the Lord and His Word.

May this book redirect Christian mothers back to seeking the Lord in our parenting. As a result, may the Lord regain His territory, and re-stake His flag to fly proudly on the family battlefield, as it should.

We, as Christian moms, are a powerful influence. When I consider us as a force for God's Kingdom, I am awestruck at the potential. Time and time again, I see groups of people in this world that unite and do amazing, unbelievable things as one movement of people. They rise up as one force, claim an identity, and passionately embrace a cause. The world is forever changed, for both good and bad, because of impassioned people.

So, what about us, Christian mothers? Aren't we a group of people on a defined mission? As a group of mothers, are we rocking this world by raising the next generation of believers? I don't think so. Can you imagine the national news reporting on the significant influence that Christian mothers have made on our society because we have been willing to radically lay down our lives to raise our kids?

I wanted to call this book, *The Battle Cry of All Christian Mothers*, but I chickened out. It sounded too haughty. Yet that pipe dream still rattles around in my soul. I just know that if we Christian mothers fully grasped our calling, our potential, and our influence, we could set the world back on its heels.

Introduction

We knew it was going to be a girl. The whole family eagerly anticipated the arrival of this precious addition. The arrangements had been made. The crib was in place. Her newborn baby clothes were all washed and neatly folded in a new dresser purchased just for her. The infant carseat was securely in place. We had been waiting for this day for nine months. We dreamed about what it was going to be like to raise four beautiful children. After many hours of prayer, all the monthly doctor appointments, and marking forty weeks off the calendar, we were definitely ready for the arrival of our little girl.

The day before she was due, I had a doctor's appointment to see how things were progressing. During his routine evaluation, the doctor noticed that my blood pressure had elevated slightly (it had been normal throughout the pregnancy). Since I was forty weeks along in the pregnancy, and the baby looked healthy and ready, the doctor decided to admit me to the hospital and induce labor.

Things progressed as planned to the "pushing" phase of delivery. We all watched the baby monitor as her heart rate fluctuated with each contraction. The medical staff explained that her umbilical cord was probably wrapped around her neck, but they reassured us that was somewhat common. I remember them telling us that about one out of three babies have their cord wrapped during delivery. As everyone's eyes were glued to the monitor, I continued to try to push her out. On one of the contractions, her heart rate dropped. Only this time it did not rebound.

In a split second, it became an emergency situation. A different doctor happened to be doing some paperwork outside the door of my room. He immediately stepped in to volunteer to vacuum her out, but to no avail. Within seconds, they were rushing me to an emergency C-section. Even though I was ten centimeters dilated and exhausted from already pushing, I clearly remember sitting straight up in bed and grabbing onto the doorjambs to help the hospital staff maneuver my bed through the doorways. Everyone soberly understood the gravity of the situation, myself included.

The anesthesiologist winked at me and whispered, "You're going to be okay. We'll get her." At the same time, a nurse stood over me listening through her stethoscope for a heartbeat. As I desperately sucked in the anesthesia, she announced to the frantic medical crew, "I just got a faint heartbeat." Somehow, I knew that I had to get to sleep for them to get her out as fast as possible. Then, all I remember is darkness. Complete darkness.

Motherhood is a beautiful thing. There is nothing like holding your newborn for the very first time. Words cannot describe that moment; the connection between a mother and a baby is instant and strong. Yet I've heard it said that the most beautiful artwork is created through pain.

I woke up to a completely different kind of darkness. As my eyes adjusted, I took in a small, dimly lit recovery room. My dear husband stood over me with tears running down his face. He was so choked that he could barely speak. I asked my love, "What's wrong, Honey?"

He gently held my hand and said, "We lost her."

I was completely stunned. I couldn't believe it. I kept asking, "How? What happened?"

Time after time, Steve would patiently go through the details with me as I tried to make some sense out of my confusion. How he heard the doctor order the medical staff to get him away from the door. How he stood there anyway, frantically watching all of it unfold before his eyes. How they abruptly sliced me open and quickly grabbed the baby out. How they rushed her to a corner of the room and desperately worked to revive her. How the doctor came out to him in tears and stumbled out the words, "Pray for your baby. We're trying to get her back, but it's not looking good."

The medical staff all urgently continued to try to bring her back to life. Twenty minutes passed as they frantically worked to save her. They eventually all stood motionless over her. No one tried to revive her anymore. They turned and slowly came out to Steve, with tears in their eyes, as they told him that our baby had died. Steve consoled them and told them that it was okay, and that they had tried as hard as they could. The whole time I was lying on the table, oblivious that my life would never be the same again.

Time seemed to slip away. They kept me drugged. I am still not sure whether it was because of the surgery or because of the heartache. I remember asking the same questions repeatedly: "How much did she weigh?" and "What color were her eyes?" I'm not sure what I was really thinking. I suppose I was just trying to grasp it all. Collecting the facts about her was the only way I could try to understand what had happened.

I was in utter disbelief. Even before the next day dawned, while it was still dark outside, the hospital staff that went through it all with us started slowly showing up in our room to console and comfort us. They each felt the extreme tragedy of it all. A healthy, 8 lb. 4 oz. baby dying from a cord accident was extremely rare, even for the people who had been delivering babies for over twenty years.

It was officially determined that our baby, Brea Grace Nelson, died of a cord accident at 1:05 a.m., on December 5th, 1998.

I kept asking to hold her. The nursing staff would gently wrap her in a pretty blanket and place her in my arms. I would sit there and snuggle her, looking at her, not knowing what to do. I tried to take pictures, but I wasn't sure if that was the right thing to do. It was so surreal. For the first few minutes, holding her was so comforting and sweet, but it would slowly turn into heartache. Her stillness and lifelessness were almost unbearable. I would hug her and hold her close, gently whispering to her as my tears would fall on her tiny little face. Yet there was no response. She didn't wiggle. She didn't breathe. She was completely silent and non-responsive to my tenderness and my warmth. There was no life there. She was gone.

I repeatedly and desperately prayed for God to bring her back to life. I knew, and was fully convinced, that God could do that. Believe me, I begged God to do that for us — for our story to be the miracle story where God's name would get amazing glory because of how He had brought our baby back to life. I promised Him that I would tell the whole world if He gave her back to me. God heard my prayers, but He said, "No."

She was a perfect baby in every way, but she was in another place. In tears, I would call the nursing staff to come take her away, only to turn around and call for her an hour later. Eventually, the staff started hesitantly asking me if I was sure I still wanted to see her. At first, I was bewildered and confused. Of course, I wanted to see her. Then I realized that she was starting to look different. Death was starting to visibly take its toll on her. So, I stopped. It just became too hard to hold her and see her like that. I desperately wanted her to snuggle up to my chest. I wanted to nurse her so badly.

I remember the gray skies, the snow gently falling, and the Christmas lights on the trees outside my hospital window. Even though the world seemed so peaceful outside, my world was unraveling in slow motion inside those sterile, white walls.

Sometimes being a mother can be hard. God has called you to walk a long journey. This journey may involve some severe blows to your faith. It may involve the shattering of your heart. Guaranteed, it will involve the breaking of your will. Yet, through it all, God is painting a masterpiece on the canvas of your life. In the end, it will be a piece of glory and beauty. My world was shattered that day. I've never been the same woman. Yet it was another step in my journey as a mother. Brea Grace was an intricate piece of the masterpiece that required the shattering of my heart. I'm so pleased to have been her mother.

Positioning Yourself

This book is, almost certainly, going to be challenging for you. In those early years, as I wrestled through laying down my life for this cause, I went through a lot of internal turmoil. I remember countless mornings sitting on my couch, in my robe, trying to catch my tears before they fell on my old pink Bible that rested on my lap. But God saw me through. He's not finished with me yet. I still have my challenging days, moments of desperation, and times of doubt. However, God has grown me into a different woman as I have pursued Him.

I pray that as you approach this book, you would prepare your heart to hear from God, and that you would be touched through what is shared here. Don't skim any of this material, as each and every detail has been placed with lots of prayer, thought, and even tears. May *your* Savior speak to *you* through this small book as I share with you my experiences and the heart that God created in me during my beautiful journey as a mother.

How you position yourself as you begin to read through this heart journey is going to radically affect the end result of reading this book. Understanding the basis from which I write to you is equally important. Therefore, be assured that I am writing to you as a mother who interprets all of my experiences through the filter of my relationship with the Lord. I cannot separate myself from my relationship with the Lord. My relationship with the Lord has everything to do with my mothering. Likewise, my mothering has everything to do with my relationship with the Lord. When I first became a mother, I wanted to position myself to align with my primary goal of following

Christ. The choice to follow Christ has unquestionably influenced my interpretation of motherhood. Am I slanted and biased in my interpretation? I am sure that I am. Hopefully, though, my slant and bias will bless you.

After mothering for eighteen years, the one thing that I can positively tell you is that mothering is way bigger than you are. Your mothering will require more out of you than you could ever muster from your own strength. The demands of raising even one child have pushed every mother I have ever known beyond her abilities, skills, and talents. Every mother I have ever met has been forced beyond her patience, forgiveness, and perseverance. All of that usually comes to pass before the baby ever blows out the single candle on his or her first birthday cake.

No woman I have ever met is prepared to be a mother. Even if you had a perfect mother whose example you could imitate, you are not fully ready for what lies ahead of you. Even if you were the oldest daughter who spent your life watching your younger siblings, having your own child is different. Even if you have a degree in child development or have always had a longing to be a mother, your mothering will require things from you that you are not knowledgeable about or equipped for. You will have experiences that shock you into complete humility and brokenness. Although I have a strong desire to equip my own four daughters for motherhood, they will not be fully prepared. They each will have to walk their own journey, full of personal trials and victories. As much as anything else, I want them to understand and accept that part of their future. They are going to need God to make it through life, no matter what they end up spending their days doing.

Neediness

With that being said, the level of neediness that I experienced when I became a mother was shocking to me. This neediness literally accosted me at the arrival of my firstborn son. Within forty-eight hours of delivering my first baby, the hospital informed us that we were ready to go home. In the eyes of the staff, we were adequately prepared for this moment. After all, they had taught us how to bathe our baby, care for his umbilical cord, and nurse our baby (although I soon found out that their amount of training in the nursing area was insufficient for what I would later need). Finally, they confirmed that we had a carseat in our vehicle. Then they released us to be the official parents of our baby.

Steve and I headed home with our precious son. It was late afternoon. Steve got everything unloaded from the car as I nursed our baby. We ate dinner. The evening hours faded away. Around ten o'clock, Steve said, "Well, Honey, I should probably head to bed. I have to work tomorrow."

Exhausted, I responded, "Well, what about me? What am I supposed to do?"

Steve patiently replied, "Well, I don't know. Can't you put the baby to bed and come to bed with me?"

Flustered, I said, "I don't know how to do that. He's already nursed, but he won't settle and go to sleep when I put him down!"

Steve sympathetically said, "Well, Honey, I don't know, but I probably should head to bed since I have to work in the morning."

I felt completely helpless. After all, it was my bedtime too! I was also going to need to get up the next morning and take care of our little baby. I needed *my* sleep too. Not knowing what to do, I stayed up and worked hard to try to settle my little newborn to sleep, not having a clue how to do that. But, truthfully, I felt slighted! You see, we hadn't had this marital conversation. We hadn't had the conversation where we divvied up the sleeping hours and responsibilities that were needed to take care of our new little baby. After all, this was going to be a fair distribution, wasn't it? He was the son of both of us, right? In theory, the answer was *yes*; but in practicality? I could immediately tell that this was going to look a great deal different than I had anticipated.

Incidentally, as I sit here and write eighteen years later, I smile. Time sure changes one's perspective! When I brought my last couple of babies home from the hospital, I felt very differently when it came time for everyone to go to bed. Steve would say, "Well, Honey, I should probably head on to bed."

I would say, "Yeah, you should go to bed, and take all of those kids with you! The baby and I will be along shortly."

Off my family would go. The house would quiet down as everyone settled in for the night. I knew that the moment the rest of the family awoke in the morning, I would have to share my baby with everyone again. So, I would curl up in a chair with my little newborn, and we would just snuggle. Miraculously, the baby would immediately drift off to sleep. It's crazy how that never happened in the early days when I so desperately wanted the baby to go to sleep! But I wouldn't rush off to bed to get my much needed sleep. I understood that this memory would quickly pass. I wanted to capture every precious moment I could with the incredible gift that the Lord had just given to me! I would sit and admire and praise the Lord for the precious little life that I was holding. Yes, time sure does change one's perspective. Yet in those early years of mothering, I was stockpiling incident after incident where I felt overwhelmingly needy and helpless.

๑๛๑๛๑

It's Spiritual Work

As I look back, I now know that motherhood takes more than a particular collection of skills and abilities. Motherhood is spiritual work. Perhaps a spiritual dimension encompasses motherhood because it is all about relationships. The relationship between you and your husband greatly affects your mothering. The relationship between you and your child obviously plays out in your mothering. You might wish that I could just make you a list of formulas that you could plug into your home scenario, and everything would work. However, one thing I have found through all of these years is that there are no formulas. Motherhood is not about formulas. Although motherhood does include certain concepts and ideas, it is far more about relationships.

Yet the most significant relationship in my mothering has been the one between my Lord and me. You see, motherhood is about faith. My motherhood has been about me putting my faith and trust in God to see me through this journey. That's why I believe that motherhood is spiritual work. As the years pass, I am more and more convinced that at the very core of motherhood is a spiritual element that a mother is forced to address. Certainly, one option is to ignore it. Yet, even in ignoring it, a mother is simply choosing to brush it under the rug. The way that a mother deals with the spiritual dimension of motherhood ends up defining her journey, more than she could ever imagine.

Honestly, I have no ideas or encouragement for the woman who chooses to do motherhood on her own strength. I can't begin to imagine how to do that. I've also never, not once, seen a mother do that successfully. I've seen many mothers try to do it in their own strength, but I've never seen one succeed.

However, I can direct you to what I know to be true, reliable, and trustworthy. I can even point you to Someone who can help you far more than I can. That person is my Savior, Jesus Christ.

❧❧❧❧

How can a relationship with Christ truly make a difference in motherhood? Is it really more important than your relationship with your husband, or your relationship with your friends, or even your relationship with your kids? What does that relationship really look like? How can you know for sure that you have that kind of relationship with God?

Well, let's start with us. All of us have secrets in our pasts. Shameful secrets. Mothers are no different; we have them too. More often than not, these secrets begin to eat away at our souls. We are in quite a predicament. We try to love and focus on our children, but at the same time our secrets shame and haunt us daily. All of our attempts to make up for or forget about our secrets, fall short of truly eradicating them once and for all. These haunting secrets are most likely, our regrettable, most embarrassing sins. When I say *sin*, I'm talking about anything that we have done or said or thought that offends God and separates us from Him. The Bible says that all people have sinned and have fallen short of God's standard (Romans 3:23). That includes you and that includes me. God says that He can't stand to be around sin (Habakkuk 1:13a). Our sins are actually the very things that separate us from God. If we didn't have our sins, we wouldn't be separated from God.

Even more so than us, God is extremely relational. In fact, through the Trinity, we see that God is relational at His core. He has relationship with Himself! God also created *us* to be very relational beings. He created us with the specific purpose of participating in an intimate relationship with Him. To make His plan work, He gave us the option to love Him or to reject Him. This is called free will. Unfortunately, our sins have broken our relationship with God—the very thing that we were so carefully crafted to take part in.

God, in His love, has sought out to mend that relationship. Romans 6:23a says, "For the wages of sin is death." Just like someone is paid an hourly wage for the work that they accomplish, we earn death for the sins that we have done. Unfortunately, this death is not just the natural death that comes at the end of our lives, but it is an eternal death – an eternal separation from God (2 Thessalonians 1:9).

Sin is like a fatal disease. We can't get rid of it. Yet God can't allow it to contaminate heaven. So the only way to deal with it is for us to be separated from God forever. But that is not the end of the story. There's hope for our broken relationship with God.

God is love. His unrelenting love drove Him to provide a way to let us out of our dilemma. He sent His son, Jesus, to come and fully pay the death penalty for each and every one of our sins, including all of our shameful secrets that haunt us. With the death penalty taken care of, we can now freely experience that first relationship with God again.

There's one dimension that still affects our relationship with God. Our free will still remains; God has still given us the opportunity to choose or reject Him. The way that we choose Him is to accept the payment that Jesus made for our sins. However, if we choose to reject Him, the death penalty remains to be filled. When we allow Jesus to pay for our misdeeds, He deals with everything—the most atrocious, the most private, the most minute, the most prolific. His death on the cross so thoroughly covered over our sins that we no longer have to be separated from God.

> 1 John 4:18 There is no fear in love; but perfect love casts out fear, because fear involves punishment, and the one who fears is not perfecting in love. (NASB)

It is because of God's love and the love that Jesus demonstrated on the cross (Romans 5:8) that we no longer have to fear the punishment that we rightly deserve.

Because of this, we can fully release our shameful secrets and the stuff that eats away at our souls. We can live without being haunted by our pasts! Can you imagine how much easier mothering would be without carrying around the shame of our pasts?

God has completely freed us from all of it. All we have to do is accept the gift that He freely gives. When we do that, we can fully embrace that intimate relationship with God and experience Him as we were created to. He not only provides complete freedom, but He continually strengthens and draws us closer to Himself. That's incredible news for any mother, isn't it? There is no better gift in the world than to be freed of our guilt and shame, knowing that we stand forgiven and accepted before God.

That opportunity to accept what Jesus did on the cross for your sins is available to you right this minute. If you want to stand forgiven and accepted before God from now on, all that you have to do is confess that you have done wrong, and believe and accept that Jesus paid for your sins. If you are at that point in your life, pray a simple prayer to God telling Him that you accept what His Son, Jesus, did for you and that you want to follow Him with your life. We can now confidently begin this incredible adventure with Christ as our Savior, Leader, and Friend.

Establishing Your Vision

Thinking back on my motherhood journey, I had to start by hammering out my vision of what a mother is. In Matthew 12:34, the Bible talks about "the overflow of the heart." In Proverbs 4:23, Solomon tells us to "guard your heart, for it is the wellspring of life." What is happening in your heart, and in your head, greatly impacts your vision of motherhood.

Let's do an overhaul of your vision. There are critical biblical truths that a mother needs to understand in order to create a vision. Each truth holds a key to understanding and accepting motherhood before God.

- Will you consider humbly and prayerfully going through these truths?
- Will you consider not moving ahead in this book until you feel like the Lord and you have worked through every truth laid out here?

Although it might be grueling work, the profound significance of our motherhood warrants this type of meticulous examination of our souls.

A Season

Seasons come and go. Even if a season lasts longer than usual, like an "Indian summer," we all know that it will pass. The Bible confirms this:

Ecclesiastes 3:1 There is a time for everything, and a season for every activity under heaven.

Every older mother you meet will tell you that your children grow up in the blink of an eye. Let me tell you a little secret; they know what they're talking about and they're right. Whether you disregard or appreciate their perspective, just know that your time of influence is short.

Every mom senses that her motherhood is a season. Not only do our kids grow out of their clothes, but they also change and mature in every other way too. Your doctor has detailed charts that monitor and gauge every step of their physical growth. Your children fly through their academic grades faster than you can keep up. And your child is daily growing emotionally and spiritually as well. You're not going to have those precious children in your home forever.

Just the other day, my oldest daughter asked me if I was planning to go to a leadership meeting that several people in our church were traveling to attend. I smiled at her and said, "Honey, I don't think I've ever been to one of those meetings. Those meetings started happening after I had your older brother. I've stayed home, all of these years, to take care of you children every single time that these meetings come around."

She looked puzzled and asked, "Is that hard for you, Mom? I mean, you *never* get to go."

Matter of factly, I replied, "No, honey. It's fine. I'm used to it."

She tried to console me, and herself, by adding, "Oh, I get it. It's just one of those A.K. things, right?"

I questioned her, "A.K. things? What do you mean, Honey?"

She smiled and said, "'After Kids' things."

I smiled back at her and said, "Yeah, it's one of those A.K. things." As we each went back to what we were doing, I realized that before I knew it, my children would be raised, and I would be attending those meetings!

Different seasons call for different actions. Each season also has its unique trials and challenges. The Bible uses a couple of different terms when it discusses seasons. One famous set of terms is sowing and reaping.

Galatians 6:7 Do not be deceived: God cannot be mocked. A man reaps what he sows.

We can easily identify the two seasons, sowing and reaping, and we can also easily see the relationship between the two. Interestingly, God warns us in the first part of the verse against our inclination to think that this principle might not always hold true.

When we read those words, we have to caution ourselves to take this truth literally and precisely in every situation, including our mothering. From the way that God worded this verse, it sounds like we must be easily deceived to think that what we sow does not affect what we reap.

How applicable to our mothering! It is easy to see the relationship between sowing and reaping in our mothering, isn't it? A mother sows and reaps. Most of us are in the season of sowing; our children are still growing. We are planting, investing, and depositing into their souls. Only *after* the season of sowing comes the season of reaping. When a mother's time of reaping comes, we rejoice and delight in the harvest, as displayed in our children's lives.

Growing up in Iowa, as a farmer's daughter, I saw my father work through the seasons year after year. Our whole family life seemed to operate around what season was happening. Dad, as well as every other farmer in Iowa, would engage in different tasks depending on the season. In early spring, I remember seeing all of the farmers out in their fields, working the soil with their plows. They were preparing their fields to be planted. Then the big planters would come out of storage. The farmers would carefully plant their seed into the prepared soil. Through the summer months, the farmers watched and maintained as healthy of an environment as possible in order for the crops to grow and mature.

My favorite season, though, was harvest time. It was almost magical. There always seemed to be a nip in the air with the first signs of winter approaching. I remember the fields glowing golden with grain ready to be harvested. As it was with most farmers, my dad often raced against the weather to get the crops harvested before the first snowfall. As one of six children, I remember standing on the couch watching out the window for Dad's tractor and wagon to appear at the crest of the hill down the gravel road. When we saw his lights coming, we knew we had just a few minutes to get ready to run down to the grain bins. We would scurry around throwing on our coats, boots, hats, and mittens. We would then race down the hill to help Dad unload the grain from the wagons under a harvest moon. It was truly unforgettable.

In the same way, I sense that I am entering a new season of my mothering. Although I am still very much in the season of sowing with my little ones, the first hints of harvest are in the air with my older children. You see, my life is marked by two year periods. At first, I was blessed by bringing home a precious newborn every two years. Now, my older kids will start leaving the home at the same rate. My oldest son could very well move out to go to college within the year. I call this upcoming season, "losing them off the top." I admit that I am a little saddened about it all. On the one hand, I am excited for them. Yet I am going to miss each one of them so much. But I know God is leading us through it all.

So I will walk this next season remembering how harvest time was magical as a young farm girl. As I write this, I choke back the tears. Although I can still remember those majestic golden fields of harvest, I know that now those golden fields are going to be represented in my children's lives. My heart sometimes quietly ponders our future without them. The bedding will finally be perfectly matched and the beds neatly made for weeks at a time. I will miss walking on all of the crumbs on my kitchen floor. The toys will be neatly stored in a box waiting for grandchildren to come and enjoy them. When Steve and I go to bed, we won't get to tuck in any little children and gently kiss them goodnight. Even though Steve and I love each other dearly and enjoy spending time together, I know we will miss having our precious children live with us.

Galatians 6:9 Let us not become weary in doing good, for at the proper time we will reap a harvest if we do not give up.

I won't carry on about this, but I must say that I am a very proud mother of my eight precious children. From one mother to another, let me reassure you that harvest season is coming. Until then, we treasure our time with them. And we press on in our all-important, sowing season and fully rely on God's amazing wisdom and grace.

With each one of your children, you only get a short season of sowing. As a mother, you have to capitalize on the opportunities that the season brings. Your time is now. This opportunity won't come around again with your child. Life is continuing to march on, one way or the other. You might feel like you're missing out on the excitement. You might feel like the world is passing you by as you rarely get showered and dressed before noon because you are busy caring for your baby. Let me assure you that you *are* experiencing life. You are experiencing true life in its most beautiful form right there in your pajamas. It's not exactly how you dreamed it would be, is it? You might not realize it yet, but these days of your life will end up being the most influential days that you will ever have! Your time is now, dear mother. Don't miss it!

My oldest son, Blaise, took a history class at a community college this past semester. One afternoon, we were hanging out in the kitchen talking after he got home from class. When I asked him what the instructor had covered in class, he said that she had told about Rosa Parks. Since I had forgotten some of the most fascinating details of the story, Blaise recounted it to me. I was speechless.

Rosa Parks, often called "the mother of the Civil Rights Movement," lived in Montgomery, Alabama in the 1950s. At the time, the city of Montgomery enforced segregation laws on the public transportation system. Black people were required to give up the preferred bus seats to the white people. Rosa Parks had just gotten off from a long day at work and was headed home on the bus. When it came to one of its stops, a white man came aboard. He strode over to her and demanded that she give him her seat. Though it was required by law for her to move, she refused. The bus driver called the police. She was arrested and taken to jail. She was soon released with the help of her friends and family.

This sparked what became known as the Montgomery Bus Boycott, the first major civil rights demonstration in our country. Led by a young man named Martin Luther King, Jr., most of the black community began a massive boycott of the bus system. They had one goal, and that was to force the city of Montgomery to desegregate the bus system. Well, the community made a plan. They banded together to prepare to boycott. The plan required elaborate cooperation and teamwork. They operated in shifts. As some people needed to go to work, those who were coming home gave them rides. The community came together to help in taking care of one another's children so that parents could still work. That same year, several men, like Emmett Till, had been brutally murdered. In addition, the Ku Klux Klan was marching in the streets of Montgomery. The whole scenario was risky and dangerous for the people of Montgomery.

The boycott went on for a week, and neither side budged. The city refused to even consider banning their law on segregation. The first week flowed into the second week. Weeks slowly became months. Six months passed and nothing happened. Seven months... eight months... unbelievably, a year passed and neither side budged. During the whole boycott, nobody had any idea what the outcome would be. But Rosa and her friends continued to endure the tiresome and dangerous stance as a unified group of people. The city refused to back down. Not only was this a pressure on the black community, but the city of Montgomery desperately needed the fares from the whole community in order to help fund the transportation system. The stakes were high for both sides.

Finally a year and a half after beginning the boycott, the city of Montgomery, Alabama, was forced to back down. The entire city had literally gone bankrupt in their stubborn attempt to maintain segregation in the trans-portation system. All of the hardships and frustrations had finally paid off and the community had finally accomplished a small, albeit painful, victory on the grueling road to desegregation. As a result of the bus boycott, the issue of segregation gained national attention, and the Supreme Court eventually declared it unconstitutional.

Rosa Parks and the community of Montgomery persevered in this boycott because they had a greater purpose in mind. We also need to be steadfast because we have a greater purpose in mind! We need to see that, just as Rosa Parks understood that her time was then, our time is now. We need to rise up with the same determination and resolve that Rosa Parks did. As in their situation, we do not know what the road will require or what will happen along the way. But we do know one thing; our time is now.

God's Gift

God has given you many amazing gifts indeed. But one of the most spectacular gifts that He gave you is the gift of each one of your children. I know that you love your children. I don't doubt that. But in the depths of your heart, do you see your children as gifts? Maybe you are not sure how you would truthfully answer that question. Let's think about a gift for a minute. A gift is something that is highly valued. A gift is often rare or unique and treated with special care, kind of like a treasure. Treasuring our children as gifts from God is central to us embracing our call to be mothers.

Sadly, our culture has spoon-fed us lies and false notions about the value of motherhood. From the time we were little girls, we received the world's message that devalued the role of the mother. The Women's Movement spent a tremendous amount of resources trying to convince women that their value was in their accomplishments and talents. Our society has embraced and promoted this mentality to the devastation of the family.

Think about how the majority of our society, including many Christians, regards children in general. One time, I remember going into a restaurant with my husband, my mother-in-law, and my eight children to have dinner. As the hostess seated us, the man in the table right next to us loudly and annoyingly exclaimed to his friend, "Oh, great! All of these children are going to ruin our dinner." When he said this, my back was turned to him as I was helping one of my little ones buckle into his highchair. When I heard him, I slowly straightened up and turned around to face him. I just stood there looking at him, letting the awkwardness of the situation take its full effect. Steve, realizing what was happening, slowly and cautiously (but still allowing the moment to play out) said, "Ka-athh, come on, Honey. Come sit down. We need to figure out what we are going to eat."

I know that this is not exactly the godly response you would like to see from me. I am sure that there were other, more appropriate, more gracious, and more effective things I could have done or said. But in the moment, I was offended at his response at the sight of my children coming toward him. This man was saying this about *my* children, in front of *my* children, and loud enough for all of *my* children to hear! I did sit down, but not without making my unspoken point very clear to him.

My children did beautifully during the whole meal. There wasn't one bit of disturbance or chaos with any of the eight of them. As I calmed down, I was proud of my little gang. I even softened, ever so slightly, to the man. As he left, he caught my eyes. He apologetically smiled and nodded his head slightly as if to say, *You're right. Your kids were great.* Admittedly, disobedient children in a restaurant *can* make eating out an unpleasant experience. But have we really gotten to the point in our society that at the sight of eight children, we are disgusted and immediately assume they are going to be an annoyance and inconvenience? Quite honestly, we have. Our society sees them as burdens rather than gifts.

Think about a different situation. When a woman tells her parents that she is pregnant, she is telling some of the most important people in her life that she is expecting

God's gift! Some parents are thrilled. Those daughters are the lucky ones. Unfortunately, women are often hesitant, even afraid to tell their parents! Why would a woman be afraid to tell her own parents that she is pregnant? Why would she anticipate that her parents would be disappointed rather than excited? Could it be because children are often not viewed as gifts? Some pregnant mothers have heard responses like, "How are you going to afford a child?" While it is true that children are a financial commitment, that initial gut-level response sends a strong message implying that a child is primarily a financial burden. Or some of you might have heard, "Having this child is going to ruin your future." That response communicates that children interfere with something "more important," namely your personal future. Tragically, some of you might have even been encouraged to abort your child by your own parents! These responses reveal that there are many people who devalue children and motherhood, even within our own families and churches.

Truthfully, deep down inside, you may actually agree with some of these reactions in certain circumstances. You may have even had some of those responses when you heard that a sister or friend was expecting. We've all heard of women getting pregnant in less than ideal circumstances. Still, we ought to have a correct view on this as well! A woman's circumstances must be separated from the value of her unborn child. The circumstances might be unfortunate, but the child is not. The more that we can separate the circumstances from the value of the child, the closer we are to understanding God's heart toward children.

What do we do with these typical responses to children? Not only do they affect us when we hear them, but they undoubtedly affect us *now*. We have carelessly allowed these ideas and notions to settle into our thinking and jade our view of children.

You are a mother now. You are now trying to do the right thing and be a good mother. Yet these seeds of pretense have been planted in your heart. It takes intentional effort to erase and refute these seemingly harmless, negative views of children. Our society has fallen so far away from God's perspective, that we actually have to force ourselves to see children as God sees them – a gift.

જીજીજી

God unmistakably reveals His heart for children in His Word:

Psalm 127:3 Sons are a heritage from the Lord,
children a reward from him.

Children are a direct, tangible reward from the Lord, which He bestows on us. Do you see the enormous difference between the two views? The world tells us that children can be a mistake, an accident, or even a punishment. Yet, here are God's terms: children are a reward from Him. Even the last two words, "from Him," are weighty and powerful. Christians rarely mention children when they talk about their rewards from the Father. Instead, they talk about how God has rewarded them with financial gain, a wonderful job, or even a great deal on something at the store. Yes, it is good and right for believers to acknowledge and praise the Lord when they sense that God has shown them kindness and grace in any way.

Yet, honestly, it seems like many people view children as a reward only at the time of a baby's birth. At the birth of a beautiful baby, we all excitedly acknowledge what a blessing and reward the child is. The "beautiful reward" then takes an astonishing turn for the worse within the first two years of a child's life. They go from being called a "reward" to being labeled a "terrible two"!

How easily we forget! We don't grasp the reward that God has given us through our children. God's Word has to be our anchor of truth that keeps us grounded in God's view of children. When I look at God's Word, I see that He has personally rewarded me with every single one of my children, despite what I am told by my culture! Although it has meant thousands of diaper changes, years of interrupted nights of sleep, and never-ending intrusions in every area of my personal life, God has made Himself clear: *Your children, Kathleen, are My personal reward to you!*

God has illustrated a very clear picture of the specific reward of our sons and of our daughters.

Psalm 144:12 Then our sons in their youth will be like well-nurtured plants, and our daughters will be like pillars carved to adorn a palace.

Sometimes, I envision these descriptions very vividly. I imagine my four sons as well-nurtured plants, maybe something like well-nurtured oak trees. When I researched the typical trunk diameter of a mature oak tree, I found that they could be as large as nine to ten feet across! People are drawn to the magnificent strength and beauty of a solid, mature oak tree. A fully mature and well-nurtured oak tree can handle fierce storms and pressures. In the same way, I imagine my sons being fully mature and being able to handle the fierce storms of life. I know that they will still be affected by the challenges of life, but hopefully, the storms will not break them. I imagine my four solid oak trees being able to provide protection and shelter for others who are not as strong. This picture gives me something tangible to pursue as a mother for my incredible sons. This is the reward that you can anticipate with your own sons.

God lovingly provides me a different, but just as beautiful, description of my daughters. Based on the preceding verse, my four daughters are described as "pillars carved to adorn a palace." Two words come to mind when I think of the pillars of a palace: strength and beauty. Interestingly, those are the exact two words that came to mind when I was thinking about a solid, mature oak tree! When you look at any picture of pillars on a palace, it is obvious that they were constructed for two distinct purposes: to beautify the palace and to provide support to the building structure. Every picture I have ever seen of pillars shows them tall, straight, strong, detailed, and breathtakingly beautiful. Yet they weren't there just for ornamental purposes; they were made for a very specific purpose - to support the building. One of my dear friends recently showed me a book that she found about palaces. She and I had been talking about this verse that describes our daughters as pillars. In this book, there were several pictures of the ruins of famous palaces. In every single picture, many of the pillars were still standing, even hundreds of years later.

Transfer that image to your daughters. Obviously, they will be beautiful, but they are also part of a critical support system. Imagine that people would have confidence in them and depend on them to build something magnificent. Those pillars are my precious four daughters; my daughters are my reward from God. To grow our sons into strong oak trees and build our daughters into beautiful pillars takes incredible vision.

Missing the True Value

Not only do we mothers miss the true value of our children, we also miss the true value of our motherhood. Most mothers tend to operate from one of three inaccurate models of motherhood: a picnic, a juggling act, or a frustration. Although each one is common and widely accepted in our society and even in our churches, none of them is a biblical perspective of motherhood.

A Picnic

The first model of motherhood is what I label, "Every Day's a Picnic." The mother who functions within this model believes that the most important thing she can offer her kids is fun and fond memories. Sure, all of the rest of life still needs to happen, like the laundry, homework, and chores. But this mother feels like she is truly being the best mom she can be when she makes her child's life fun. After all, in her mind, she owes it to them. This is their childhood; they deserve to have fun. Having fun is her way of demonstrating love to her children. In fact, the more "picnic" events scheduled on the family calendar, the more she believes that her children will feel loved and valued. This mother usually determines the value of a week depending on how many fun things are planned. Interestingly, this mother tends to avoid conflict because it is "no picnic." Therefore, her enforcement of boundaries and correction usually lack in consistency and effectiveness. The one thing she wants her kids to remember is all the "picnics" that they had growing up that she sacrificed to make happen. Treating life as a picnic takes the focus off of equipping children for their futures. We live in a harsh world that needs men and women of God who are well trained.

A Juggling Act

The second model of mothering is "A Juggling Act." The mom following this model tries to do it all. Imagine a mom sitting Indian-style, having about eight arms, kind of like an octopus. In each arm, she is masterfully juggling something. Each "priority" that she is juggling is the same size and weight. The following things are carefully balanced on each octopus arm: her laptop that she uses to keep up with the outside world, a spatula which she uses when she whips up amazing meals, a hand weight that she exercises with every day, a credit card that she uses to buy the latest fashions, her cell phone that she uses to call important people, a glass of wine to allow herself a little indulgence, a steamy novel that she daily gets lost in, and lastly? A little baby rests in her remaining extended arm. This mother has her heart divided by many things. She is simply juggling that baby along with everything else. When the child demands attention, she meets his needs, but she then quickly redirects her attention and heart back to all the other "important" things that she enjoys juggling. This mother uses warnings and threats as much as possible to discipline her child. After all, she doesn't want to be bothered with the work of biblically disciplining her child. The child is left neglected and ignored, feeling like an intrusion in her own mother's life.

A Frustration

The last model of motherhood is when it is viewed as a "Continual Frustration." The mother who holds this view hopes to get a break from her children as often as possible. She is different from the juggling mom because she operates in a constant state of frustration with her children. She's not trying to juggle other things; she is just frustrated that she has to "waste" her life taking care of her children! Imagine her standing in the kitchen, trying to talk on the phone. Screaming children come running through the kitchen dragging the barking dog and crying baby along with them. The whole scene is widespread chaos. She has a frazzled look on her face, with both of her hands pulling out her own hair! She does enforce discipline in her home, but she only does it in anger when she hits her boiling point. Incidentally, she hits her boiling point frequently and dramatically. Basically, her kids are constantly rattling her cage. She feels trapped and like she is the victim of her own children.

Which one of these models do you tend to operate in? Which model did your own mother operate in? All of us who read through these descriptions of motherhood quickly realize that not one of them is how God views motherhood. Possessing any of the three of these models of motherhood will result in you being ineffective, struggling with feelings of guilt and regret. Although it is true that mothering can definitely include all three of those elements at times, none of those models reflect God's design of motherhood.

Shaping a Life

Motherhood is shaping a life, like the potter shapes the clay.

> *Jeremiah 18:1-7 This is the word that came to Jeremiah from the LORD: "Go down to the potter's house, and there I will give you my message." So I went down to the potter's house, and I saw him working at the wheel. But the pot he was shaping from the clay was marred in his hands; so the potter formed it into another pot, shaping it as seemed best to him. Then the word of the LORD came to me: "O house of Israel, can I not do with you as this potter does?" declares the LORD. "Like clay in the hand of the potter, so are you in my hand, O house of Israel."*

Just as the Lord takes us in His hands to shape us, so we mothers shape our children. Imagine a mother at a potter's wheel. She takes the raw clay, her child, in her hands. She feels the soft touch of her Savior's hands as they cover hers. She senses the Lord's guidance, as she carefully handles the moldable clay. The clay is gray and unformed. It is messy. She recognizes that the process is going to be time-consuming. She carefully centers the clay on the wheel, appreciating the significance of this foundational step. She is aware that her mishandling of the clay could mar her finished product. She understands that the strength of her masterpiece comes in her ability to correctly center the clay on the wheel in front of her. She begins to massage the clay with one hand on the inside and one hand on the outside. The clay softly molds under her hands.

And so begins the long process of shaping her child's life. She will spend endless hours sitting at the potter's wheel, massaging the clay. As she works out any air bubbles that appear, and restores cracks when she sees them, she senses that she is forming the foundation of her masterpiece. All the time, she feels her Lord's hands guiding her, applying more pressure here, nurturing more tenderness there. In the same way that the potter shapes clay into a beautiful vase, motherhood is shaping a life into a masterpiece for the Lord's glory.

Your child is your heritage. You get the opportunity to define your branch on your family tree. Christian parents can come from incredibly broken and shattered homes. Yet they have to choose to raise their children differently, before the Lord. They might feel overwhelmed that their family tree has produced nothing but heartache and pain up to this point. However, imagine a fresh, tender, bright green branch coming out of a knotted, gnarled tree. The tree is still alive, but it is so deformed and twisted that its dominating characteristic is its ugliness. The tiny green branch is the first sign of life on the tree after so many years of deformation. People stop in amazement; they actually see signs of life coming out of something so ghastly. Mother, it may be the same way with your heritage. Whether it is or not, within your grasp is the opportunity to create a branch of your family tree that brings incredible glory to God.

The Bible uses a different analogy to describe your heritage. It depicts it in the form of a letter that you write. Imagine your children's lives as letters written by you. These letters are addressed to the world, to be read by everyone.

2 Corinthians 3:2-3 You yourselves are our letter, written on our hearts, known and read by everybody. You show that you are a letter from Christ, the result of our ministry, written not with ink but with the Spirit of the living God, not on tablets of stone but on tablets of human hearts!

Your children are your primary letter to this lost and hopeless world. We can't choose to write a different letter and tell the world to disregard the letter scripted through our children's lives. This is the letter that God has assigned you to write. As the above verse states, this letter is written with the very Spirit of the living God! We cannot offer anything less to this broken world! My eight children are my heritage, my branch, and my letter to this crazy, lost, and hopeless world. I understand that. As the years pass, my heart enlarges with this reality.

I realized more and more the significance of my life being offered up for my children as I had more children. After we had delivered our seventh child, I had tallied up five C-sections. My dear doctor, a good friend of ours by this time, met with Steve and me because he wanted to share some thoughts with us. We greatly respected him as a doctor and a friend. We went to our appointment, eager to listen to his counsel. As the meeting began, we asked him for his medical expertise on me having a sixth C-section and having another baby in my forties. He patiently addressed each issue, stating any risks that might be related. As the meeting went on, we sensed that he had something else to say. Although there were certainly some medical risks to consider, he had something more human and tender on his heart—as a friend rather than a doctor.

Finally, our doctor admitted to us that he wanted us to consider not having any more children. When we pressed him to explain, he confessed that he didn't want anything bad to happen to me or to one of my babies. He thought we had such a sweet family and that we should count our blessings. Before we left, we again asked him a variety of specific questions about any medical concerns that he might have about me. He told us that it wasn't *that*; he just wanted nothing bad to happen! As he put it, "The seven beautiful children that you have would make any parent proud! You should just count your blessings." He was right...on one hand. But we knew that our children were our heritage.

We went home. Steve and I were touched by his genuine concern and love for our "little" family. We understood his perspective about us being blessed. We wholeheartedly agreed. However, God had been building convictions in our hearts. As our family had grown, our convictions also grew.

Time passed. A few years later, we moved down to El Paso, Texas, to help start a church plant. As we settled into our new city, we heard about a renowned, high-risk obstetrician that practiced in El Paso. I made an appointment. We hadn't conceived yet; we just wanted a second opinion (specifically regarding any medical risks) about what our good doctor in Colorado had told us.

We explained our whole medical history to this new doctor, including our three miscarriages and the loss of Brea. We specifically asked him whether or not he thought it was wise if we tried to conceive one more child. He listened intently. As it is with most doctors, he had no perspective of the eternal value of a child or a parent's spiritual heritage, nor did we expect him to. Consistent with his training, he was looking at the medical facts. I would be in my forties having my sixth C-section. Although I had done remarkably well with each one of my C-sections, everyone agreed that it was a major operation and not to be taken lightly. He finally spoke. He told us that he had no real issues about us trying to have one more child, but he was not comfortable recommending a seventh C-section beyond that. As much as two non-medically trained people could, Steve and I understood the risks. We had already experienced some of the most painful "risks" of delivering babies.

We appreciated both doctors' advice. We carefully prayed through it all. But there was one huge difference between our perspective and theirs. No matter what the medical details were, our children were our heritage! We deeply believed that. As much as they were our heritage, we knew that God had entrusted us with His heritage too. We prayed. In faith, not knowing what the future held, having talked through all of the medical risks with two reputable doctors, we had our eighth child, via my sixth C-section, in 2006. God has blessed us with eight healthy children. For that, we are so thankful. We are so pleased with the heritage that God has entrusted to us.

Our influence does go beyond our own heritage because we belong to another family that expands beyond our biological family. We belong to the body of Christ. The children who come out of my home and the children who come out of your home are literally the next generation of believers. Our children are God's upcoming army. Our children are the ones God is going to use to reach out to the lost and dying world. Being mindful of this, are we equipping our children to be skilled members of God's army to reach the world? God's heart is for every believer to be an active member of His plan. He clearly laid out His mission for each one of our children. They should center their lives around this high calling.

Matthew 28:19-20 "Therefore go and make disciples of all nations, baptizing them in the name of the Father and of the Son and of the Holy Spirit, and teaching them to obey everything I have commanded you. And surely I am with you always, to the very end of the age."

These are the very words of Jesus when He was here on the earth after His resurrection and before He ascended back into heaven. These verses in Matthew 28 are often referred to as the "Great Commission." It is God's mission statement for every single one of His believers. In light of the mission He gave us, we should direct each one of our children to focus every aspect of their lives around this mission. For example, they should pick a career that carefully fits into this mission statement. In addition, we parents should only focus on skills and abilities that will help further this mission. When we comprehend that we are literally raising the next generation of believers, we fully understand the potential that their lives possess. God seems to want all of their potential, skills, and abilities funneled into one purpose—accomplishing the Great Commission.

God wants the same thing for us mothers as well. When we look at the Great Commission in light of a mother's life, we have to be able to see its application. God's mission for every believer is to make disciples. God's mission is to teach our disciples to obey everything that He has commanded us. Many mothers can clearly imagine how to live out the Great Commission in their city, but not in their own homes. They seem to get stuck on the "go" part.

I have experienced the full delight of the "go" part of the Great Commission within our family life. First, we have had the opportunity to go, and be part of starting two different churches in two different cities! And, second, we have had amazing experiences going out and sharing the gospel at the parks and malls in our city, as our children have gotten older. Those experiences have been incredibly exciting and life-changing for both our children and us! Mothers aren't exempt or forgotten in living out the Great Commission; they just live it out differently depending on the season of family life they are in. As God has called our children to live out the Great Commission, He has called each of us mothers to also fully live out the Great Commission within our homes, as we raise up our disciples.

The Exchange of Lives

Ironically, motherhood is a veiled exchange. You're expecting it to be no benefit to you, but that isn't totally true. Granted, an integral element of my mothering definitely includes me giving up my life. So, what is the exchange part of it? From my perspective, it can seem like it is all about *my* sacrifice, *my* loss, and *my* surrender. What do I get in return? Where's my bonus? Where's the benefit to me?

This is the exciting part! In the exchange, I actually change the world! I exchange my life for theirs. My life is being used to shape eight other lives. I could never accomplish on my own what my eight children collectively will be able to accomplish with their lives. I have the opportunity to change this world, not just through my own life, but also through the lives of my eight children.

I am not boasting. This is simply the opportunity that any parent has with his or her kids. I've heard it said that, "No one can out-impact a parent." That is absolutely true. The parent gets first dibs on influencing his or her child.

Our society even has social programs like the foster system that are designed to help parents fulfill their proper position *as* parents in their children's lives. Everyone agrees that this is the right and privilege of the parent, if they choose to accept it. Dawson Trotman, the founder of Navigators, once said, "Never do anything that someone else can or will do, when there is so much to be done that others cannot or will not do." God gave me these kids. There's no going back now. They're mine. Steve and I are the ones that God wants to use to do this job of shaping their lives.

The exchange of lives is spiritual in nature. As Christ exchanged His life for ours, so we exchange our lives for our children's lives. There was a season in my mothering when I was meditating on the following passage:

> *Philippians 2:16-18 "But even if I am being poured out like a drink offering on the sacrifice and service coming from your faith, I am glad and rejoice with all of you. So you too should be glad and rejoice with me."*

As a mother, my life felt like it was literally being poured out like a drink offering, as a sacrifice. One time, while preparing for a Motherhood conference, I started searching for an image to express this feeling. I knew that the moms would know what I meant; I just wanted the perfect picture to capture what I saw in my mind and felt in my heart. As I scoured through hundreds of pictures on the web, I became discouraged. Steve casually walked by and asked me why I was frustrated. I explained what I was trying to find. As he peered over my shoulder, he told me that he thought any one of the pictures pulled up on the screen would capture what I was trying to communicate. Each picture showed water being poured into a basin or container. But I told Steve that none of those pictures were exactly right. They were all missing something that I couldn't quite express.

As I was trying to explain it to Steve, I scrolled down to the next set of images. And there it was! The perfect picture of what motherhood felt like was right in front of me. It was simple in nature, with very little color or fanfare. The picture showed water falling out of a glass vase into an endless sea of water. No shoreline was visible, just water. Nothing was catching it. No one was watching it fall. The small vase of water obviously had no impact on the vast sea of water. It was just being swallowed up by it. The water was being poured into the sea, never to be noticed or defined again, as it had once been in the glass vase.

Motherhood feels like that, doesn't it? It feels like your life is being poured out. No one is "catching" your life and your sacrifice. No one is seeing your life as you pour it out. It feels like your life isn't making any difference; rather, it is just being swallowed up by the endless routine of motherhood. That completely captures what motherhood *feels* like. Yet just because it feels like that, it doesn't mean it is true.

Now, imagine a different picture. Imagine flowing, moving, water. It never stops; it is continuous. The water is flowing with a commanding, intentional, and valuable purpose. Yes, it is water that is still being poured out. But this picture is different. Even though the water is not being caught by any container or basin, it is creating a form. The stream of water is actually creating something recognizable, perhaps the form of a precious child. If you saw this happening in real life, you would be astonished and wonder how this could possibly happen. How could moving water ever take any form without some kind of a container, especially a detailed, eloquent form? But there it is happening before your very eyes.

So, which image captures your view of motherhood? Is motherhood the image of water pouring out with nothing to catch it? Or is motherhood the image of water being poured out to create something defined and eloquent? Your view of these two images, as they relate to motherhood, exposes whether or not you believe in the exchange of lives! The exchange is spiritual—supernatural. Even though motherhood frequently feels like the first image, it is actually the second image. It is the supernatural process of a life being poured out and God creating a recognizable, brilliant masterpiece!

The choice to exchange your life for your child's life is made in your heart. Not only do you exchange your life for another, but a more intimate exchange needs to happen. The most intimate of exchanges is the exchange of the heart. If you are married, you know what I am talking about.

Proverbs 23:26 *"My son, give me your heart and let your eyes keep to my ways."*

We understand that desire for our children to give us their hearts, don't we? We totally appreciate that. We want our kids to willingly and freely give us their hearts. Sometimes, Steve and I say those exact words to our kids; we will ask one of them, "Honey, do I have your heart?" When I am asking that question, the answer is usually *no*, and the child knows it. I then tell my child that I want him or her to regroup and choose to give me his or her heart. When that child chooses to do this, he or she is tender toward my input, my correction, and my affection. When this happens it restores peace in our relationship.

Let me ask you the same question. Do your kids have your heart? When both the child and the mother exchange their hearts, it is truly powerful and life-changing.

ৼৡৼৡ

I never saw the exchange so clearly demonstrated as when the Lord made the decision to take my daughter's life. He literally chose, in all of His love and wisdom, to exchange her life that others might live. How exactly did that play out? Brea Grace was welcomed into heaven in the month of December. That following spring we started seeing a glimpse of God's plan. The churches in our community were planning a city-wide Easter service to be held at the University of Northern Colorado's football stadium. To make a long story short, Steve and I were asked to share our story of Brea at the service. The gospel went out. Hundreds of people heard the story of God's redemption and love as demonstrated through our daughter's death. Steve had several other opportunities to share our story throughout that following year. We know of several people that came to know Jesus and put their faith in Him after hearing Steve tell our story of Brea Grace. On the day that the Lord takes me home to live with Him forever, there will actually be people in heaven who are there because they put their faith in Christ after hearing Brea's story. God has used our daughter's story to draw people to Himself! Amazing! Her life had a lasting eternal effect on others. Her life was exchanged that others might live—eternally live!

The Lord impressed on me that my life was the same as Brea's. My little girl and I were doing this exchange thing together. The Lord used her little life to show me that He wanted the same for my life. Just like Brea Grace, He wanted me to exchange my life that others might live.

John 12:24 "I tell you the truth, unless a kernel of wheat falls to the ground and dies, it remains only a single seed. But if it dies, it produces many seeds."

The Scripture calls us to fall to the ground and die that others might live. Who are the others? Well, for me personally, it definitely starts with my family. Interestingly, the verse uses the word "unless." Unless a kernel falls, it doesn't bear fruit. Someone has to die. The Lord, unmistakably, spelled this out for me. He spoke into my spirit, *Kathleen, unless you die, you remain a single seed. You yourself will live and remain. But if you willingly fall to the ground and die, your children will live!* That was a profoundly powerful moment in my heart! Yes, Brea and I both were created to die so that others might live.

I treasure the precious lesson that the Lord taught me through her life. I love my dear Lord for giving her to me and helping me see His plan for my life through her. God is an amazing, loving, tender, thoughtful, and kind Lord that I completely trust with my whole life. He led me through all of that and has healed my broken heart. He has given me a true peace that only comes through Him and His love. I dearly love my little Brea Grace. One day I will meet her and live with her forever. Until then, I will press on and live out the truths that the Lord taught me through her life.

Your Calling

The moment your first child was born, your calling changed. He did more than just give you the title, "mother." He gave you a calling. He gave you a "trust." The Bible addresses those who have been given a trust.

1 Corinthians 4:2 "Now it is required that those who have been given a trust must prove faithful."

When God gave you your child, He committed someone to your care. He entrusted your child's care to you, and He commands you to be faithful to that calling.

Christian mothers are a special group indeed. Not only have we been given our individual "trusts," but we are collectively raising the next generation of believers! Our individual "trusts" make up the army that He wants to use to reach this lost world!

Even though there are countless Christian mothers, recognize that your own journey might be a lonely road. The hope that all Christian mothers would rise up and change the world is a right and noble hope and something worthy of our prayers. However, I have had to come to grips with the fact that God has called me to do this, regardless of whether other Christian mothers decide to do the same. Even if I walk the road alone, I still must walk it. At the core of this decision lies only one person, and that person is me.

Yet I have not forgotten the few Christian mothers along my journey that have taught me profound lessons, often without using their words. They taught me by their example. In the same way, remember that we mothers are impressionable and teachable. Much learning occurs through watching one another's example. Although it might seem that you are the only mother embracing your calling, remember that God can stir and inspire other mothers through your example.

> 1 Corinthians 15:58 "Therefore, my dear brothers, stand firm. Let nothing move you. Always give yourselves fully to the work of the Lord, because you know that your labor in the Lord is not in vain."

I can't hope to rally all of my Christian friends to join me in this calling. Nor do I have the time to rally everyone. From my experience, I have found that this road can be sparsely populated. Every once in a while, I have found a friend who has shared a passion for this "extreme" commitment to motherhood. More often, I have felt that I am walking this journey alone. I think we all feel that way to some degree. After all, no one comes into my home and rescues me on a daily basis. I am pretty sure that you would agree that most days it is just you and God. It can sure feel lonely, can't it?

I had to lay down my expectations of every Christian mother joining me. The Lord gave me a verse to help me relinquish my expectations of others. In the book of John,

Peter and Jesus were walking along. Peter noticed John, one of the other disciples, was following them. The Scriptures say:

John 21:21-22 When Peter saw him, he asked, "Lord, what about him?" Jesus answered, "If I want him to remain alive until I return, what is that to you? You must follow me."

I was busy looking around at other Christian mothers and evaluating what they were doing. The Lord rebuked me with His Word and said, *Kathleen, what is that to you? You must follow me.* From that time on, I realized that whether or not the road was crowded or abandoned, I was choosing to walk it anyway. Jesus' words, "You must follow me," commanded me to keep my eyes on Him and stop worrying about everyone else. This journey is between God and me—no one else.

৵৵৵৵

When God gives any of us a calling, He desires our whole heart in obeying Him.

God illustrates how much He wants our complete surrender in the following verse:

Mark 12:30 "Love the Lord your God with all your heart and with all your soul and with all your mind and with all your strength."

God is asking for our whole hearts.

Romans 12:1 "Therefore, I urge you, brothers, in view of God's mercy, to offer your bodies as living sacrifices, holy and pleasing to God—this is your spiritual act of worship."

His desire is for us to offer our whole selves as living sacrifices. When we offer Him our lives, we commit an "act of worship." Most of us only see ourselves worshipping God when we are singing to Him! It is rare to find someone who understands that sacrificing their life is actually a meaningful form of worship.

1 John 5:2-4 This is how we know that we love the children of God: by loving God and carrying out his commands. This is love for God: to obey his commands. And his commands are not burdensome.

Translated to our mothering, God wants us to embrace our motherhood wholeheartedly by loving His children. In order for there to be any fruit in our mothering, we have to consciously make that choice. At the end of my life, I want to be able to say that I did my very best. I was diligent with the calling the Lord put on my life. I was not distracted from my mothering. I did not prioritize my house, physical beauty, finances, career, friends, or extended family over my own children and husband! Rather, I want to be able to say that for many, many years, I faithfully gave my most gentle side, the best of my love, the fullness of my attention, and my most tender nurturing to my husband and children.

Mothering is far more about your heart than about your actions. In fact, your actions are a direct response of what is stored up in your heart.

James 2:22 You see that his faith and his actions were working together, and his faith was made complete by what he did.

It is challenging to evaluate the condition of your heart, isn't it? In my own attempt to tangibly measure the condition of my heart, I realize that I can bring two different hearts to my mothering. After reading the following verse in 2 Corinthians, I came up with labels for those two different hearts: a heart to mother generously, and a heart to mother sparingly.

2 Corinthians 9:6-7 Remember this: Whoever sows sparingly will also reap sparingly, and whoever sows generously will also reap generously.

In context, this passage is discussing two different hearts toward financial giving—either generously or sparingly. Yet I appreciate the application to my mothering. There are all kinds of indicators that a mother is generously giving her heart to her kids. Some indicators that show me that I am mothering generously can be if my house is not perfectly kept, dinner is not ready on time, and I feel completely spent at the end of the day. Even though those things can be positive indicators that we are prioritizing the correct things, we can feel guilty or frustrated by them. When all three of those things happen in one day, we often feel like it was a bad day! We go to bed frustrated and determined to not let that happen again the next day!

That misguided thinking is a tell-tale sign that we haven't trained ourselves to value what is truly important. These kinds of things can be frustrating, but they actually might need to happen to attentively take care of your children. We need to resign ourselves to these types of inconveniences and be peaceful, knowing that we are doing the right things. Our frustration is misplaced because a tidy house and timely meal is not more important than tending to our children. Sometimes our feelings are just that. Feelings. They need to be corrected and redefined, not accepted in their true, pure form. If we are not careful, we can just march along with our emotions misleading our souls! We have to be intentional in our mothering. Prioritizing our children over our house and our meal plan, is a good, right, and appropriate indicator that we are mothering generously.

Even after all this time, I still have to remind myself that these things are not necessarily bad. When my life gets a little messy because I prioritize doing the right things, God is pleased. That means that I need to choose to be pleased as well. I do realize that an untidy house, a late meal, and an exhausted mother could have nothing to do with mothering generously. I also realize that having a tidy house and a timely meal could have everything to do mothering generously! Neither situation is a definite indicator, one way or the other. As is true everything else, it all revolves around your heart more than your actions. In the end, generous mothering often means that our lives get disheveled; we have to accept that as part of the package.

One of my goals in mothering is, "no regrets mothering." I definitely don't want to look back on my years as a mother and have regrets. It is true that in some of the little things, I already have regrets. I do wish I had read to them more. I wish I had introduced them to more learning opportunities. I wish I had taken them to the park more. But I consider those things as the insignificant things. It is impossible to do everything. I need to do the main things and do them well. Steve often encourages me by saying, "Honey, you are majoring in the majors. Keep doing it, Babe."

I can't do everything that I want to do with the kids. That leaves Steve and I to carefully evaluate and strategize about the things we want our kids to excel at. These are the critical things we never want to have regrets about. Sometimes, I hear mothers talk about how they feel bad that they didn't do certain activities for or with their children. Oftentimes, the very things that they feel bad about are not "major"; they are minor things. Unfortunately, I rarely hear moms worry about neglecting the right, important things that we need to accomplish as mothers. For example, I hear moms wishing their kids were able to be involved in more extracurricular activities, but I rarely hear moms agonize over the deficient spiritual development of their children.

As mothers, we all have to let some things go; we just need to make sure that we let the right things go and capitalize on what truly matters. In faith, we need to determine these critical, nonnegotiable, major pieces of our parenting. We evaluate and strategize on what those major "pieces" are as we consistently position ourselves before God in prayer.

Each one of these truths, carefully pieced together, can create a framework for a biblical vision of motherhood. However, this framework will require more from you than just merely reading about it. You will need to breathe life into it. From my experience, only one thing can breathe life into a vision: your heart. Before God, you will need to breathe life into your vision by giving it your whole heart. Put your faith and trust in Him who called you to motherhood in the first place—your Savior.

Rebuilding Your Identity

My vision for my mothering is so intricately tied to my identity as a mother that I had to wrestle out both of them simultaneously! Let me ask you a question. Can you see yourself living out this vision? If you can't see yourself in the middle of this vision, then your motherhood is going to be an endless struggle. Along the way in life, each one of us developed an identity of ourselves. Whether it was based on fact or simply our perceptions, we each saw ourselves in a certain way. We dreamed of our gifts and talents being used and valued. For most of us, the idea of motherhood was not what we had arranged our identity around. Many of us hoped to one day "be a mom," but we didn't rationally cultivate our identity to revolve around our role as mothers.

Is God calling you to something different than what you were planning? Is He calling you to something new?

Isaiah 43:19 "See, I am doing a new thing! Now it springs up; do you not perceive it? I am making a way in the desert and streams in the wasteland."

I realize that He is talking about Israel in this verse, but God has the same desire whenever He is doing something new in any of our lives. God wants us to understand that He is doing something fresh in our lives, and He is thrilled about it! In order for us to join God in His excitement, we have to willingly let go of how we used to view ourselves and our futures.

As I have become an older mom, I have grown to dislike, and actually disagree with the familiar question, "What do you want to be when you grow up?" This question is commonly used to encourage or provoke a child to think about their future. Even in Christian homes, parents will casually ask this question when engaging with their children about possibilities for their future. Maybe I am being overly analytical (although I must say that I am rarely, if ever, accused of such a thing!), but this line of thinking is completely unbiblical and encourages our children to dream about their futures, absent of God's leading and direction. How were you raised? Did you hear those words? I know I did.

For most of us, one of two scenarios played out in our childhoods. Some of us were encouraged to dream big and to use our "full potential," picking a career that would magnificently demonstrate all of our gifts and talents. When this conversation happened, we instinctively knew that we were supposed to gaze off into the horizon, proving that we were lost in the incredible possibilities that our futures held. The career that we suggested was supposed to be something big, something amazing, and something that would change the world forever. Appropriate responses might have included something like being an astronaut, the first woman president, or a Nobel prize winner. After answering the question "correctly," our parents would snuggle us in their arms and say, "You can be anything you want, sweetheart!" From that experience, we were affirmed that this was the way to "believe in yourself" and plan for your career. Let me ask you one question. Where was God and pursuing His will in that conversation?

Then, there was the other end of the spectrum. Some of you might have been raised with no such encouragement to dream at all when it came to your future career. Your parents might have never had that conversation with you. Perhaps, the exact opposite happened—you were told that you would amount to nothing and would never be good for anything. When you thought about your future, you had no hope that you would ever do anything that truly mattered or impacted the world. Let me ask you a question. Where was God and pursuing His will in that conversation?

❧❧❧❧

Which of those two scenarios is more tragic? Interestingly, most of us would claim that the second scenario is the more tragic of the two. And, indeed, it is heartrending. If you experienced that growing up, I sympathize with you. How painful. I am sure that you feel ill-prepared for the noble and meaningful role of motherhood.

But would most of us even call the first scenario tragic? If we are honest, many people would not. In my mind, both scenarios are equally tragic, just in different ways. Regardless of which scenario you were raised with, neither one of those scenarios equipped you for the position that you are in today as a mother.

Think about the first scenario with me. What would have happened if you dreamily gazed off into the horizon and answered, "I want to be a mother." Trust me; most parents would have corrected their little girl's "dream." The parents would have directed her down a different, "more significant," pursuit of her future. At least they would have added more career possibilities to her dream. How many of you were taught that if you were "just" a mother, that you would be doing something noble and meaningful with your life? I don't have my hand up either.

Whatever our experience was, neither scenario inspired us to connect to the Lord and follow God into His plan for our futures. Frequently, Christian parents naively put abilities and passions at the center of the discussion about career possibilities with their children. Our public schools do that; they administer interest-based and ability-based assessment tests to help direct teens down a certain career path. The only thing that the Christian parent seems to do differently is to make sure to carefully fit God into the *wording* of it all. Strangely, Christian parents *do* tend to put God into the center of the conversation when it revolves around who their kids will marry, but not in the career conversation.

I shake my head in confusion over this one. In the end, Christian kids often end up disappointed because their dreams were impractical and unrealistic as viable career options. Only then does the parent turn their children to God and put Him at the center of their planning for their career possibilities. It seems a little late and a lot more agonizing than starting with God as the center in the first place. I wonder, if God was at the center of those conversations as young girls, would more of us have ended up with the answer *mother* in the first place?

Matthew 6:33 "But seek first his kingdom and his righteousness, and all these things will be given to you as well."

A Puzzle

No one told us that we were creating our own puzzle when we were growing up, but we were. We were creating an identity puzzle. It was an identity that would highlight our personality and uniqueness. With every experience, we were forming pieces to fit into our identity puzzle. When something bad, painful, or shameful happened, we tried to throw those pieces away. Sometimes we succeeded. None of us were necessarily gifted at this puzzle-building business. We just worked from what was said to us, and about us, by people bigger and "more important" than us.

We didn't know what we were doing. We just felt the need to do it. Something deep inside us wanted to be accepted and loved. Somehow, we knew enough to know that our identity puzzle was all tied into getting those needs met. Unknowingly, we were trying to place each puzzle piece on a board. Yet we couldn't even see the final design! Some of the pieces didn't seem to fit perfectly, but we forced them in the best we could.

Growing up, most of us weren't really looking to God and asking Him to show us what puzzle pieces He wanted us to use to build our identity. We were going on instinct. By the time we reached adulthood, we each had developed some form of an identity puzzle that we owned and operated from. Most of us were just getting comfortable working with our identity puzzle when the unthinkable happened. We had our first baby!

❧❧❧❧

Your first baby came along and literally tossed your precious identity puzzle right out of your tight grasp. Puzzle pieces went flying everywhere. You were completely flabbergasted. You had worked so hard to create this identity; it had taken years to create! Yet your baby turned your puzzle, and your world, upside down in a day. If you hadn't been holding your baby in your arms, you would have frantically gathered up the pieces and started rebuilding your precious identity. You came home from the hospital with your cherished baby and your identity pieces safely tucked away in a side pocket of your new diaper bag. While you were enduring the first few months of nighttime nursing, you often thought about the moment that you would be able to dig out your precious puzzle pieces and rebuild the identity that you knew and loved.

Finally, that moment came, one afternoon while the baby was napping. Full of anticipation, you found your diaper bag and situated yourself on the floor. You wanted to be able to enjoy every puzzle piece all over again. After all, it had been so long since you had touched and experienced them! You reached into the pocket where you had carefully tucked them away. Shocked, you found that they had slipped out and had fallen to the bottom of your diaper bag! You tentatively pulled out your treasured identity. You were horrified to find the puzzle pieces soaked in spilled milk, with soggy teething biscuits pasted to them, and reeking of soiled diapers. In despair, you tried to salvage them. There on the floor you sat, desperately trying to piece your identity back together. However, the pieces were warped, peeling, and rancid. They were completely ruined and didn't even fit together anymore. You were stunned. Your once-treasured identity was ruined.

Starting Over

No one told us that our old identity would be ripped right out of our hands, never to be recovered again. But that's exactly what happened. Now what? What are we supposed to do?

God is standing right there; ready to help you take that next step. God wants you to look to Him to recreate an identity using His board and His pieces this time. This time, He wants you to do it His way. God has a new plan for your life. If it is God's plan for your life, then you are left with one good choice to make: you must make it your plan.

Something profound did change that day, as you viewed the ruined pieces of your identity. God swapped your identity. He gave you a different, unfamiliar puzzle board. Not only that, but He also exchanged your precious puzzle pieces with a new set and wants you to start all over again. Here you are, responsible for another life that you love so much, and trying to rebuild your own identity at the same time. The funny, and yet not so funny, part is that God has only handed you one piece to begin with! Remarkably, that piece resembles Himself.

These new puzzle pieces, the ones that God has given you, seem to be completely unrelated to your importance and significance. In fact, they seem to be prioritizing everyone else's needs instead of yours. What is God doing with you? Does He have a plan? Is He intending to forget you in this new identity? That's what it may feel like as your new life as a mother begins to unfold. Yet one thing that you know for sure is that God is calling you to redefine your significance.

Redefining is scary. Are you willing to let God do that in your life? Are you willing to let God take you through the process of reexamining and reevaluating your significance with the sole purpose of changing it?

❧❧❧❧

I remember my stubborn attitude when God first confronted me with the need to redefine my identity. After all, hadn't God given me certain talents that He wanted me to use for His glory? Honestly, I seemed so "gifted" in my own mind. Frankly, this mothering role was, indeed, a limited expression of my gifts and talents. One of my abilities that I particularly enjoyed was my ability to have meaningful communication. I especially delighted in thought-provoking, stimulating, two-way conversations! Motherhood was throwing a big wet blanket on this wonderful ability of mine. I was limited to cooing and mono-syllable sentences. Reciprocal communication was even more limited! (Eventually, I learned to appreciate my babies' smiles and sparkling eyes. They kept me carrying on these one-way conversations day after day, for years!)

Incidentally, this personal struggle was all interconnected to my value. Although I didn't voice it, I was wrestling with whether or not motherhood was a worthy enough cause to sustain my need to feel valuable. In the early years of my mothering, the answer seemed to be a booming *no*. In fact, mothering seemed to aggravate my daily pursuit of self-esteem. As hard as I tried to maintain my self-esteem, mothering zapped all possibility of it. I had nothing left as I lay my head on my pillow at night, often letting my tears fall as I drifted off. The deep sleep that I thought I so badly needed constantly evaded me. God allowed my sleep to be interrupted no matter how hard I prayed. In those early years of mothering, trust me when I say that I learned how to pray. No doubt about it. I was desperate. Somehow, I knew that how I resolved this inner conflict was going to have a profound effect on my family.

Everything that I knew to be familiar and stimulating was gone. Were there any thought-provoking experiences left in my days? Not so much. Much to Steve's dismay, I would try to fulfill my need to have meaningful conversation the second he would walk in the door from work. Now, if you don't know Steve, he's a quiet guy. Every day, he uses up all of his word-capacity before noon, whether he is with people or not. His desire to come home and rest didn't exactly line up with my agenda back in those early days. I wanted meaningful relationship, and I thought he was just the guy to give it to me.

Well, Steve was not cooperating with my plan. And "my plan" was the precise problem in my life. God was calling me to surrender, and I wasn't listening. That proved to be a very unhelpful and extremely frustrating approach to take toward God. In all of His love and grace, He made it crystal clear to me that He wanted me to surrender.

Expired Dreams

Surrendering seemed so hard. I would have had a bleak outlook had I not believed that God had something better planned for me. I remember the Lord dealing with me on this issue on my couch one morning when I was having time with the Lord. While I was sitting there in my robe, He gently made it clear that all of those dreams that I was still trying to fit into my little world weren't going to happen. In fact, the Lord gave me a word to describe those dreams. He told me that they were expired!

Now, what do you do when you find an expired coupon at the bottom of your purse? Well, you throw it away. But what if it was really valuable? What if it was worth a lot? What if you had every intention of using it? We all know that none of that matters if the coupon is expired. When something is expired, that defines its value. "Expired" terminates any value that it might have had at one time.

In the same way, when I became a mother, all of my dreams and goals for my personal life became expired. I didn't realize it then, but they had an expiration date on them, much like a coupon does. They were valid for a certain period in my life; that period was now officially over. I observe so many mothers holding onto expired dreams, trying to fulfill what they wanted for their lives before they had their little ones! I see mothers desperately trying to utilize their talents and gifts at the expense of their children. I see mothers trying to fit their career goals into their lives as mothers. What they don't realize is that not only did God give them a new identity, but He also gave them a new set of dreams and goals. They just don't see them yet.

At this phase in my own life, God was giving me no wiggle room on this front. The question wasn't what He wanted me to do. The real question was if I had the courage and faith to obey Him. And I present that same question to you: Do you have the courage and faith to embrace God's new dreams for your life?

ক৵৵৵

By this time in my life, I had experienced enough of God's goodness and mercy that I knew how things would work out. I had also seen people in my life who had decided to do things their way, instead of God's way. I recognized the hopelessness in that plan. I had even deposited some years of personal heartache from trying to do things my own way, instead of God's way. The lasting effect of the pain and sorrow from those experiences still made me shudder years later.

Yet I was in a big dilemma. I had gotten my master's degree in Speech Communication. I had taught communication courses at the college level. I had also enjoyed some "productive" years of women's ministry. I had seen "fruit" in my life as I invested in people. In fact, people seemed to like me! To be honest, sitting in the rocking chair nursing my baby within the four little walls of my house seemed to be a dismal use of all that God had given me!

I was stuck in a hard spot. Both paths looked scary. In the end, I closed my eyes and, agonizingly, released my grip on my plan and my identity. In God's grace, I took that step of faith.

Years passed. I plugged away. I never had much time to realize or reevaluate that big decision. The babies kept coming. I continued to get more and more buried in the demands of motherhood. Then, one night I was sitting at my computer on the eve of my fortieth birthday. One of my dear friends had written me an email to wish me a happy birthday and ask me how I felt about my life on the eve of this milestone. I remember just sitting at the computer, staring at the screen. How did I feel about my life? Forty years had passed. That was a long time. By then it was likely that half of my life was spent.

As I began to write, I choked back the tears. At the time, the Lord had been encouraging me with a verse in Deuteronomy.

Deuteronomy 7:9 Know therefore that the LORD your God is God; he is the faithful God, keeping his covenant of love to a thousand generations of those who love him and keep his commands.

I sat there humbled by how much God had done in and through my life. I reflected back to my childhood as a little girl with pigtails growing up on a farm in Iowa. That seemed like an eternity ago. Now, here I sat decades later. I had become the mother of six beautiful children. I had married a man far better than I deserved. I wrote to my friend, "It is a humbling privilege to have experienced God's incredible grace and kindness for forty years." I sat

78

there with no regrets. I was pleased beyond words. I could have wished for nothing more in those forty years. All of my dreams, some of which I didn't even know I had, had been fulfilled because the Lord had watched over me, protected me, and blessed me. That night was a milestone in my faith journey that I will never forget. Sitting there all alone, I truly understood and valued all that God had done in my life.

God knows what He is doing with us. When He asks us to relinquish our identity, He doesn't want us to go dig up another identity to lock onto. In fact, I realized that the problem with how women develop their identity was that they put their identity in their roles, not in their relationship with Christ. God taught me that I had an identity outside of any role that I might have been fulfilling. My roles could change over the years, but I would still have the same, consistent identity. When my children are grown, I will still have the same identity that I have today. If Steve passes away and I am a widow, my identity will not change.

In His "identity restructuring" process in my life, God showed me that He wanted me to define myself solely based on what the Scriptures said. As I scoured His Word collecting verses, I didn't find a single verse that defined our identity based on our roles. Granted that there were plenty of verses about how to live according to different roles, like as a wife, a widow, or even as a woman. Yet every single one of the verses instructed me to live according to my relationship with Christ, within that particular role.

So, what is the function of our roles? Our roles are simply avenues to live out our identities. I learned so much as the Lord began to rebuild my identity. In this process, I expected it to be about me. However, the Lord taught me that it wasn't just about myself, but about His body of believers and what He has called all of us to. Even though my new identity was not based on my role as a mother, I could clearly see how to live it out in my mothering.

Although I had accepted Jesus as my Savior as a young girl, I had never really pieced together His calling for me as a believer. I had received merely a sketch of my purpose growing up in the church, but I could not have laid out a comprehensive picture of the identity that God had given to every believer. That became more important to me as I became overwhelmed with mothering my children. My identity was not about what He had called me to as a person with my particular gifts and talents. God calls every single one of His followers to certain things, unrelated to their gifts and talents. He calls all believers to obedience in every area of their lives. My situation, as a mother, is simply a role to live out God's calling for me.

The Call of Every Believer
A sacrificed life is the mark of every believer.

1 John 3:16-17 This is how we know what love is: Jesus Christ laid down his life for us. And we ought to lay down our lives for our brothers.

It was a huge wrestle for me to lay down my whole life as I carried out my assignment to be a mother. That verse ran through my mind day and night (and, since I was awake most nights, I truly mean day and night!). How was I going to get around that verse? Wasn't there any way to save myself *and* live out this verse?

Motherhood is a tremendous sacrifice, but that sacrifice is God's will for my life. It is not a sacrifice that can be managed or carefully dispensed as your flesh and emotions determine. No, it is an all-out, without-moderation sacrifice. In fact, you are trusting God to rescue you instead of rescuing yourself by your own maneuvers. Pure abandonment to my Savior and His calling on my life is what He defines as faith. Living a sacrificed life just happened to fit perfectly into my life as a mother.

God calls every believer to imitate His sacrifice.

Ephesians 5:1-2 Be imitators of God, therefore, as dearly loved children and live a life of love, just as Christ loved us and gave himself up for us as a fragrant offering and sacrifice to God.

It is effortless for me to fit "a life of love" into my motherhood. But there is an even more amazing truth that has deeply encouraged me. Even if I wasn't a mother, God would still be calling me to live a life of love and to lay down my life for others. God isn't just calling mothers to this challenge. This is what He expects from all believers.

God calls every believer to bear fruit.

John 15:16-17 "You did not choose me, but I chose you and appointed you to go and bear fruit — fruit that will last. Then the Father will give you whatever you ask in my name."

What about a believer's purpose in life? Is God's call on mothers really any more demanding than His call on every believer?

Maybe it helps you, like it did me, to know that God appointed each of His believers to bear fruit. My application of that verse had clear definition because He had given me eight children to mother; my children were going to be a significant portion of the fruit that He appointed for me to bear. He *appointed* me to bear fruit! He chose me. He selected me. Whether I am a mother or not, He assigned me to bear fruit all of the days of my life.

God calls every believer to walk their own path.

Hebrews 12:1 Therefore, since we are surrounded by such a great cloud of witnesses, let us throw off everything that hinders and the sin that so easily entangles, and let us run with perseverance the race marked out for us.

I was encouraged to realize that God has marked out a particular path for every single one of His followers. The "race" that God had defined for me was the raising of my children. This was a profound encouragement to me. God has marked out a certain, unique race for each one of us. A couple of years after the Lord showed me this verse, I was turning on the television to start a video for the children. At the time, the Winter Olympics were happening. My attention was piqued as I noticed a men's cross-country skiing competition happening. The sports announcers were discussing the features of the course that these men were racing on. It was full of unique challenges. The announcers were predicting that the first few men would be coming in about four hours after they had started! I remember just standing there watching all of these grown, physically-fit men struggle and fall *up* this particularly long, steep hill (which, by the way, wasn't even at the end of the race). Now, remember that these were world-class athletes that had been training for this event for years. But this particular "race" that was marked out for them that day, had its distinctive challenges and trials that were putting these well-equipped men to the test. I just stood there watching these racers with this verse running through my head! I got it; I totally understood the parallels with what I was watching to what I was living.

My race is hand-picked by God; His plan is for me to run this particular course. He wants me to trust Him, seek Him, and bring Him glory as I run my specific race. Although there might be some similarities, my race will look different than yours. All mothers have their own race that God has marked out for them, with its own challenges and features. Some mothers have twins, some mothers have several babies in a short time span, some mothers have physically or mentally challenged children, some mothers have all boys or all girls, some mothers have lost their spouse, and the list goes on and on.

Sometimes, women will tell me that they could never handle raising eight children. I usually comment that they don't have to worry about that unless God calls them to it. God might never call them to raise eight children, and here they are, stressing about the "overwhelming" possibility. My loving heavenly Father has hand-picked my perfect race for me to fully experience all of His goodness! Our races are going to look different. We just need to focus on the particular race that God laid out for each one of us. How reassuring this truth should be to each one of us.

God calls every believer to have the attitude of Christ.

Philippians 2:5-8 Your attitude should be the same as that of Christ Jesus: Who, being in very nature God, did not consider equality with God something to be grasped, but made himself nothing, taking the very nature of a servant, being made in human likeness. And being found in appearance as a man, he humbled himself and became obedient to death — even death on a cross!

Even in our attitude, God gives definition and boundaries. This attitude is what God calls all believers, everywhere, to adopt. It just happened to be that this attitude was extremely applicable to my mothering. It helped me to know that, no matter what my circumstances were, the attitude described in Philippians 2 was going to be the barometer of my attitude for my whole life.

God calls every believer to godly speech.

Ephesians 4:29 Do not let any unwholesome talk come out of your mouths, but only what is helpful for building others up according to their needs, that it may benefit those who listen.

A mother's speech has the same biblical boundary as for any believer. Now, I know the challenges of keeping our speech in check as we mother. We need to think about our word choice, be very careful with our tone, and even give careful consideration to the timing of our words. And, trust me; I have failed in every single one of those dynamics of my speech as a mother. Yet, the demands of raising our children don't exempt us from God's parameters for our speech. He clearly calls me to use "helpful" speech that builds others up according to their needs. No matter what my circumstances, God is still holding me to this standard.

God Called You

God enlisted me. I can't disregard my duties as a mother and choose to exercise all of my gifts in a different scenario. The result would be dreadful. For example, I can't go out and use my master's degree at the expense of being a good mom. God wants me to be a good mom first and foremost. Using my Master's degree is optional; my mothering is not. God has undeniably called me to be a mother! He has given me other gifts, talents, and interests, but they don't all have to be used at once, or even at all.

I have met more than a few moms who feel confined by the role of mothering. They are desperately trying to find life outside of their home. They feel trapped like a caged animal within their own four walls. I'm sure we can all relate to those feelings.

However, when I hear a mother express this "need" to get out of her home, it often is a symptom of her heart. It's not just a result of her personality or preference. That mom tends to wrestle with embracing her *vision* and *calling* as a mother. Those two things go hand-in-hand. If you are a mother who feels the need to get out of the house every day to avoid going stir crazy, I challenge you to examine your heart. Going outside of our homes all of the time leaves our children distracted and unfocused. It does the same thing to us mothers as well! We end up distracted and unfocused. If we are unnecessarily running errands and hustling about, we only tend to the needs of the moment with our children. There is no training going on.

In America, it is common for families to live this way from sunup to sundown, every day, 365 days of the year. "Mothering in the mini-van" has never been effective for me or for any other mother that I have ever met. Unfortunately, I see an epidemic of "mothering in the mini-van" in our culture. God speaks against this hustling and bustling lifestyle. God calls all mothers to be busy at home.

Titus 2:4-5 Then they can train the younger women to love their husbands and children, [5] to be self-controlled and pure, to be busy at home, to be kind, and to be subject to their husbands, so that no one will malign the word of God.

God doesn't just call the mothers who are homebodies to be busy in their homes. He calls each one of us to be busy in our homes, regardless of how we feel about it. There's a reason for that. He knows that we need to consistently be in our homes in order to give our full attention to the training of our children. He understands that a child's spiritual identity is developed through the routine and daily functions of a godly home.

As we remain busy in our homes, we are freed up to concentrate on raising our children. But the only reason that a woman would choose to be busy in her home would be if she understood the significant things happening in her home. She would know that God is working in her children's lives as she and her children daily live life together in their home.

There are moms across this country who need to say, "God has called me to be a mother." They need to say it to the woman they see in the mirror. They need to say it until their hearts change, until they believe that motherhood is God's will for their personal lives. Are you one of those moms? Carefully consider that your acceptance of this calling could deeply affect the fruit that comes from your home.

Mothers are a dime a dozen. There are a lot of us, aren't there? Am I saying that we should just join the masses of mothers across this country and take our place in the lineup? No! Not God's mothers. We are a special breed. We are a treasured asset to the Lord and to our families. We must realize that we bring a profound influence to our homes, our churches, our country, and our world.

Most mothers fulfill the basic duties of a mother. Yet we must be different. *How* we mother is the difference. We cannot depend of the strengths of our personality to accomplish God's agenda in our children's lives.

Godly mothering is only accomplished as we mother outside of our personality. Our strength has to come from the Spirit in our lives, not from ourselves.

Romans 8:6 The mind of sinful man is death, but the mind controlled by the Spirit is life and peace.

I have found that when I mother in the Spirit, it accomplishes God's agenda for my children. In Galatians, we read a list of indicators that God's presence impacts our lives.

Galatians 5:22-23a But the <u>fruit</u> of the Spirit is love, joy, peace, patience, kindness, goodness, faithfulness, gentleness and self-control.

I don't know of any personality type that is described using the fruit of the Spirit. We Christian mothers must not operate in our personalities; we must operate in the Spirit! As I have set this goal before me, I am amazed at how motherhood has pushed me to be the person I want to be, not the person that I naturally am.

A Life Coach

Occasionally mothers will approach me and question me about what I do in my home all day long. They admit that they are bored and restless in caring for their children. These mothers miss the momentous importance of their role in their children's lives. Mothers should daily be structuring a spiritual foundation in their children's lives.

One day, my phone rang. It was my friend from college. We hadn't seen each other for a couple of years, and she was going to be in town on business. We agreed to meet for a lunch at a cozy little Mexican restaurant. As we sat there catching up on one another's lives, she told me that she was considering changing careers and becoming a life coach. Having never heard of that career, I asked her about it. She explained that people would hire her to help them analyze their life goals and coach them on how to reach those goals. She added that a life coach didn't just address a person's career track, but it included every area of a person's life – family life, spiritual growth, emotional well-being, physical fitness, etc.

As she explained this all to me, I sat there completely stunned! She was describing my life to the tee! I came home completely exhilarated; I finally had the words to describe what I do all day in my home! Yes, I am a mother, but more specifically, I am a life coach. I am coaching my eight clients in every area of their lives in order to prepare them for adulthood.

We need to realize that the hours spent in our homes with our children are with purpose. We are responsible to equip them for life! We are literally coaching them to understand, handle, and succeed at life! Somehow our kids need to come out of our homes, after eighteen years, ready to walk their own journey of faith. When we pause to think about all that needs to happen to equip them, we should shudder. We have such a short time to accomplish such a comprehensive, grand goal!

So, that is what I am doing all day in my home. I'm not bored. I'm not restless. On the contrary, I'm on a mission! On occasion, I have moments of boredom and restlessness. But I have had to train myself to look beyond my feelings and remember my calling as a mother. After all, I have a mission; I am a life coach.

⋙⋖⋙⋖

One of the most important areas that a mother coaches her children in is their spiritual development. She needs to take the responsibility to create a spiritual environment for her children. Within the home environment, important components of her children's belief systems are first introduced, explained, and modeled. Sometimes, Christian parents are involved in churches with the hopes that church will accomplish these spiritual goals in their children's lives. This is not the responsibility of the church. The church should simply compliment, reinforce, and confirm what the parents are doing in the home. In the following verse, God explains that the spiritual lives of children should be developed in the daily life of the family unit.

Deuteronomy 6:4-9 Hear, O Israel: The LORD our God, the LORD is one. Love the LORD your God with all your heart and with all your soul and with all your strength. These commandments that I give you today are to be on your hearts. Impress them on your children. Talk about them when you sit at home and when you walk along the road, when you lie down and when you get up. Tie them as symbols on your hands and bind them on your foreheads. Write them on the doorframes of your houses and on your gates.

One of the primary responsibilities of a mother is to model how she places God at the center of her life. In doing this, she is showing her children how to do the same in their lives. The Word tells us, as believers, to put God first.

Matthew 6:33 "But seek first his kingdom and his righteousness, and all these things will be given to you as well."

Our children need to see *how* we do this. They need to see our choices demonstrating this priority in our lives. This is critically important. It has been said that these things are not taught—they're caught! We can't just show them this verse; we have to demonstrate it for them. The stakes are high; there's no doubt about that.

Children develop their faith early. Mothers get the opportunity to teach their children to revere the sacred, Holy Scriptures. Watching our attitude and heart toward God's Word places our children's hearts and attitudes under the spiritual shelter of God's Word.

As much as possible, a mother's duty is to introduce, explain, and model the Scriptures. She needs to intentionally transfer the Scriptures into the everyday lives of her children. In order for this to successfully happen, a mother needs to be personally experiencing the transforming power of the Scriptures in her own life. The kids have to see that transformation happen before their eyes in their mother's life. When they observe that, their own faith deepens.

> *Romans 12:2 Do not conform any longer to the pattern of this world, but be transformed by the renewing of your mind. Then you will be able to test and approve what God's will is—his good, pleasing and perfect will.*

How do we demonstrate a transformed life to our children? The answer is in the above verse. A mother has to renew, or refresh, her mind! I recently learned that the function of the F5 button on a computer is to "refresh" the webpage you are on when browsing the internet. Since our computers are obnoxiously slow and old, sometimes they can get stuck and need to be refreshed. I've loved this new little trick. But I've also thoroughly enjoyed the spiritual implications. We regularly need to push our F5 buttons and refresh ourselves back to a baseline of spiritual truth! As we renew our minds in the Scriptures and "refresh" in the truths of His Word, our lives are transformed before our children's eyes! They get to witness God transforming a life as they live out their childhood in the shadow of their own mother! What a priceless gift that we can give to our children!

A Discipler

Not only is a mother involved in the creation of a spiritual environment, she also devotes herself to the discipling of her children. She needs to position her own children as her primary disciples. She is conscientious to pour all of her knowledge, experience, and wisdom into her children in order for them to follow and put their trust in the Lord.

The mother needs to utilize every chance to impart God's truths to her children. While the laundry is running and the meals are cooking on the stove, a mother is using normal life to disciple her children in the ways of the Lord. She understands that everyday life is the perfect stage to show her children the love of the Father through *her* love. She knows that predictable childhood folly will happen, but she considers it an opportunity to demonstrate biblical discipline to her children. The Christian mother is well aware that biblical discipline drives out folly (Proverbs 22:15) and imparts wisdom (Proverbs 29:15) into their souls. A godly mother recognizes that within the routine of home life, there are countless occasions to instruct her children about the ways of the Lord.

❧❧❧❧❧

A Drip Line

During the process of writing this book, I went to my mother-in-law's house for a week. It was a long, arduous week, and I missed my family deeply. Although I talked to them everyday, it was hard being away from them. When I returned home, a friend of mine called on the phone to see how it went. She knows my family well and has spent considerable time in our home. As I was telling her how difficult it was for me and my family, she started chuckling. I asked her what was so funny, and she responded, "Yes, Kathleen, your kids probably did have a challenging week. They have grown up in an environment where they are used to you giving them a continual drip line of encouragement, support, and input of truth into their lives. When you went on your trip, there was a kink in their drip line, and they didn't have you continuously building into them. I bet that *was* kind of challenging for them!"

I was completely taken aback with that assessment of my presence and my absence. Yet as I got off the phone and went about my day, I was so pleased she described my influence on my children in that way. I have thought about that conversation so many times since it happened. The Lord used it to deepen my understanding of my influence in my precious children's lives. I thank the Lord that He has given me a vision. I fully embrace that I am a life coach and a discipler of my children.

Infinite Impact

A mother's impact knows no boundaries. Her impact is not confined to her four walls. In fact, those four walls actually increase the full effect of her life. When you think about it, every mother has that kind of impact. Regrettably, there are mothers who have such a negative impact, that their children seemed scarred for life. These mothers are deceived to think that their bad choices will not negatively affect their children.

I remember once having a very serious conversation with a mother about the impact of her wrong choices on her own children. I was astonished when I listened to how she had convinced herself that her drug habit was *her* problem and would have *no* effect on her children. Even though her children had literally been taken from her care, she stubbornly and foolishly held to her opinion. She thought that because they knew she loved them, they were in a safe spot, and she would hopefully get them back soon, her children would have no long-lasting harmful effects from her drug habits.

Sometimes, I think the "good" mother can be just as delusional. She can be just as convinced that her good choices will have no long-term impact on her children. She can think that even though her children know she loves them and that she provides a God-centered environment at home for them, they won't remember it all anyway! It won't have any lasting impression on them. This mother believes the lie that her right choices are unnoticed and worthless.

Every mother has to wrestle out whether she actually believes that her life matters if she spends her life within the walls of her home, mothering her children. A mother is going to be hard pressed to give her life to something that she doesn't truly believe matters. We are all driven by reward and meaningfulness in any endeavor. We mothers are no different.

> *Matthew 6:19-21 "Do not store up for yourselves treasures on earth, where moth and rust destroy, and where thieves break in and steal. But store up for yourselves treasures in heaven, where moth and rust do not destroy, and where thieves do not break in and steal. For where your treasure is, there your heart will be also."*

God understands our nature. He knows that we don't do much unless we perceive that it is to our advantage. He's okay with the idea of motivating us with treasures or rewards. He simply requests that we consider where we want to cash in our rewards—here, in the present, or there, in heaven. The verse makes it pretty clear that you can't do both; if you are cashing in on your rewards now, you aren't going to be able to cash in later.

Imagine what a mother's treasure might look like if she was collecting her treasures on earth. She might be mothering for the praise of others and to look good in front of her peers. She might be maneuvering her mothering around her goals of maintaining her own comfort and personal well-being. She might be fulfilling the duties of mothering, but she is really driven by living in her dream house and driving a car that she is proud of. The above verse confirms that her heart is not truly in her home. It tells us that you can look at a mother's treasures and tell exactly where her heart is.

You see, it truly matters what your heart is drawn to while you mother. The wonderful thing is that you have a choice of what you allow your heart to be drawn to! Let me challenge you with two indicators that reveal your heart – your schedule and your speech. Does your calling to be a mother define your schedule? Does your calling to be a mom define your speech? Here's the bold truth. If I could look at your schedule, and if I could hear your conversations, I could tell if motherhood is truly your passion and your heart. Just take a minute. What does *your* schedule and *your* speech tell *you* about your heart?

❧❧❧

My neighbors who live across the road are hunters. They are not your typical hunters; they are hunters of exotic animals! As a family, they have traveled to South Africa on numerous occasions on hunting expeditions. The first time I walked into their house, I was astonished to see all of the taxidermy of exotic animals proudly displayed throughout their home. I estimate that there were at least thirty dead animal heads hanging from their walls. My neighbors relished the opportunity to explain what type of animals they were, as it was not obvious to a novice like me. They had animals displayed that I had never even heard of! What an experience!

As I slowly walked back across the road, I reflected on the commitment that they had made in order to display all of those animal heads. I thought about the time commitment. I thought about the financial commitment. What did it cost to have dead animals shipped from South Africa to El Paso, Texas? I didn't have to do any research to know that doing so would cost a pretty penny. Then, there was the fact that they were so proud of those hunting accomplishments, that they had them stuffed and hung all over their house. They walked under those "treasures" every day of their lives. I am not saying that our neighbors didn't treasure their kids; they did. I'm sure their displays reminded them of many wonderful family experiences. But to me, the heads on the wall graphically represented the idea of treasuring our rewards.

Before I had reached my front door, my mind was reeling as I pondered what they would see as important to me if they toured our home. I promptly walked into my closet. For years, I had been meaning to hang my collection of baby pictures of my eight children up on a wall. I'm not normally one to organize and plan such things, but I had somehow uncharacteristically managed to have a picture taken of each of my eight children when they were three months old (all wearing denim, no less!). Needless to say, I haven't accomplished it for any other age, just at three months. I promptly found a hammer and hung all eight of my children's baby pictures in a crooked row. (Thankfully, Steve later lined them up properly.) I displayed them on the wall in the room right next to my front door. I wanted people to see my "trophy wall"; this was what I had invested my life in, and I wanted it displayed for the whole world to see. My children are my treasures.

Investment

Even though all of us women enjoy our material things, we are intensely driven by relationship. It seems that God has made us different in this way. All women invest in people. The critical question is who they invest in. The truth is that we typically invest in the relationships that we also get the most out of. Over the years, I've developed many friendships. Some have lasted for many years; some were just for a season. The relationships that have lasted have something in common: both of us get meaningful benefits out of the relationship.

The "meaningful benefits" part of a relationship presents a problem when we are talking about our relationship with our children. As we are raising little ones, the "meaningful benefits" for the mother seem to be a distant fantasy. That's because, to some extent, they are.

This relationship is unique. It requires more of a building process than most other relationships.

We have to look beyond the temporal lack of payoff in our relationships with our children. If you were to meet a new girlfriend and it became apparent that you were going to need to invest years of initiative, kindness, and forbearance before you could ever develop a meaningful relationship, you (and I) would probably walk away, thinking that it was not going to be worth it. We might find ourselves thinking: *if she isn't going to try, neither am I.* That's how mothering is, except there is no walking away from these relationships. The payoffs come later in life.

We know that. We sense that. We have to come to accept that. Our error comes when we try to replace and prioritize other relationships to get our needs met when we should be spending that time investing in our kids. We choose to invest our hearts into other women instead of our children. On the other hand, the Scriptures do clearly encourage women relationships.

Titus 2:3-5 Likewise, teach the older women to be reverent in the way they live, not to be slanderers or addicted to much wine, but to teach what is good. Then they can train the younger women to love their husbands and children, to be self-controlled and pure, to be busy at home, to be kind, and to be subject to their husbands, so that no one will malign the word of God.

You can see that the older to younger women relationship is explained and encouraged in that passage. All of that is good and right. Yet we need to be mothers who view our children as our *primary* disciples. We need to invest in them first and foremost. There might be room in your life to disciple other women, but not before your children, not at the expense of your children, and not in place of your children.

Years ago, a younger mom asked me to go out for coffee. At the time, I had five little ones. As we sat in the local coffee shop, she asked me if I would consider discipling her. She was very sweet as she told me how she wanted to learn from me and just glean any wisdom she could from our conversations. She reassured me that she knew I was very busy and that she would be willing to take any small amount of time that I could commit to her. She even suggested once a month if that was all I could give her.

I told her that I would love to, but I needed to talk to Steve first and that I would get back to her. When Steve and I got a chance to discuss it, I was horrified that Steve said that I couldn't even go out for coffee with her once a month. He lovingly explained to me that I had too much going on and that I was critically needed in our home working with our kids. He said there were other women who could disciple this young mom. In my heart, I knew he was right, but I dreaded telling this dear friend that I couldn't even go out for coffee once a month. After "discussing" it with Steve a few more times, I anxiously approached this friend to tell her what Steve and I had decided. My heart sank as I apologized and asked her to please understand why we had made that decision. Needless to say, she was very gracious as I explained our reasoning. A couple of months later she approached me at church. She told me that our decision taught her more than if I would have met with her monthly for the whole year!

100

Our example discipled her! We mothers often underestimate the impact of our example. Let me challenge you with a thought. Can we effectively disciple other women by our example, rather than by meeting with them weekly? I was discipled that way; I watched how other godly women lived their lives, and God profoundly used those women in my life. By living reverent, biblically-based lives, we invest in our children, while, at the same time, investing in other women.

My Little Box

In some of the earlier years of my mothering, I was meditating on the reality that the vast majority of my influence was limited within my four walls. During a conversation with a friend, I said something like, "All that I have is my little box of influence within my four walls." Well, a dear brother in Christ overheard me say that. He knew our family well and had even lived with us for a few years. He approached me later and said, "Kathleen, you need to quit saying that! That is *not* true. You have a huge box of influence with your children. You are going to rock the world for Christ with these kids, and you are walking around moaning about how little your box of influence is!"

I was stunned by his loving reproof! He was right. I was going to have a huge influence on this world, even though it was beginning from my little box, my home. I have always remembered that conversation. There is plenty of truth there for all of us. Each one of us has a huge influence which begins in our homes, with our children! Our houses may be small, but our influence is not. There's a difference between the two.

Years ago, when I was reading about the life of Susanna Wesley, the book described her influence this way:

> "Her life accomplishment was affected mainly within the narrow circle of a home in a remote and uncongenial swamp in Lincolnshire. Her activities were restricted to her family and her husband's parish. Yet she gave to the world two geniuses of the first rank: John, founder of Methodism, and Charles, one of the greatest hymn writers of all time."

Is that powerful or what? Susanna understood that she was "giving" to the world by raising her children. She probably had no idea exactly what would become of their lives, but she knew that their potential was limitless.

Let me ask you a question; What are you giving to the world? We all want to make the world a better place. In all likelihood, the most recognizable way that you and I are going to impact the world is by what we give it through the lives of our children!

Reinforcing Your Perseverance

Veggie Tales defines perseverance as "keep on keeping on." When you spin a top, it spins quickly for the first thirty seconds or so. A really good top might be able to keep spinning for more than a minute. But after that, we all know that every top starts to sputter out. As mothers, we need to be careful not to sputter out after the first little bit of our parenting. (I admit that I have lived in a world full of toys for a few too many years.) We need to be tops that reach the end of their momentum, yet keep on…and keep on…and keep on. But before we talk about keeping on, let's talk a little bit about the phase of motherhood when it is easy to spin.

It's easy to spin when you are lying in the hospital right after delivery. Granted, some of that spinning is adrenaline! Yet the hospital staff is, ideally, at your beck and call. Several professionals are monitoring and caring for you and your baby to make sure everything is okay. That wraps up the easy spinning part of motherhood—the first day or two. Then you only have 6,572 days to "keep on" spinning.

Every mother that I have ever known that didn't abandon her family somehow managed to make it through all of those 6,572 days of her child's life. They made it through one way or another. I've seen quite a diverse display of tactics that mothers use, even Christian mothers, to persevere through all of the years of motherhood.

The world offers all kinds of enticing tricks to help us cope with and handle the pressures of motherhood. Every women's magazine that I have ever picked up is filled with things to "rescue" me. The next time that you see a women's magazine, slowly flip through each advertisement and ask yourself, "What is the world trying to entice me with in this ad?" The world's temptations are undoubtedly masterminded. They stimulate all of our senses. They come in all forms. The world promises to rescue us with physical beauty, fitness, intelligence, significance, relationship, romance, ease, and comfort. Even though we seem to intellectually know that the world's tactics are temporary, ill-focused, and ineffective, we fall prey to the world's allurements day after day, year after year.

❧❧❧❧

Discerning Voices

The voice of the world is clever. It is also self-promoting and empty. I once attended a very popular Christian mother's support meeting. A good friend had invited me because she knew that I had a heart for helping mothers. She wanted me to consider joining the group to minister to all of the young mothers who were attending. Steve and I decided that I should give it a try.

What I witnessed in that meeting flabbergasted me. The leader of the group unashamedly told the fifty or so young moms that they needed to focus on taking care of themselves. She reminded them that they still had God-given dreams and goals. She warned them that no one was going to make sure they achieved those goals, except themselves. She reassured them that they would be better moms if they regularly got away from their kids and did the things they enjoy doing. These young, vulnerable moms were eagerly shaking their heads in agreement throughout this whole spiel.

I would have expected that from a non-Christian meeting. However, I adamantly felt like what was shared at that meeting was completely unbiblical! It took all of my willpower and a ton of God's grace to respectfully sit through that meeting and remain silent. As I drove home, my frustration built. I was exasperated; what a complete disservice to Christian mothers!

Someone please find in the Scriptures where God endorses any such ideas! I just do not see it in my Bible. Nothing that she shared was from the voice of God; it was the voice of the world. Maybe it sounded spiritual; after all, she did throw the word 'God' in there. However, her advice was not biblically based. There is a huge difference between the voice of the world and the voice of God. We mothers must be able to identify and discern the difference. Whose voice are you listening to?

Resisting Idols

Sadly, moms are picking and choosing from the world's bag of tricks to refresh themselves. All that the world offers us is "worthless idols."

Jonah 2:8 "Those who cling to worthless idols forfeit the grace that could be theirs."

A latte from Starbucks, an exotic weekend getaway, a trip to the gym, a shopping spree, a juicy novel, a manicure, and the latest fashion boots from Zazooland can all fall under the heading of "worthless idols" at times.

Of course, problems happen when you are relying on this bag of tricks to get through motherhood. When the money runs out to pay for the gym membership, when the car breaks down and you can't run to Starbucks, or when something interferes with plans to get away for the weekend, you are left disappointed. If you reexamine that verse in Jonah, you'll see the devastating consequence of that path. You forfeit God's incredible grace! The very thing that you cry out to the Lord for, you willingly forfeit!

All the while, our little children are looking up into our eyes wanting relationship and love. Instead, our eyes are turned away from them. We aren't looking down; we are looking out. We are looking out to the world to get our own needs met. We don't consciously put those things above our children, but that is often how it plays out.

Moms who cling to worthless idols substitute them for the incredible, life-changing opportunity to experience God as their Rescuer. Most Christian mothers don't experience God as their true Rescuer because that can only happen when they abandon their worthless idols. Corrie ten Boom, a Holocaust survivor and renowned Christian author, captured this truth in her famous quote, "There is no pit so deep that God's love is not deeper still." Mothers feel the "deep pit," but instead of looking for God to rescue them, they look to the things of the world to deliver them.

1 Peter 2:11 Dear friends, I urge you, as aliens and strangers in the world, to abstain from sinful desires, which war against your souls.

The Bible warns us to stay away from worldly desires. The result of pursuing these types of desires is that they wage war against our souls! I've been there; I can give testimony and confirm that this verse is accurate. When I pursue the desires of this world, they war against my soul by battering my encouragement and hope. I am left feeling even more discontent and restless than ever. I hate it when I do that. Yet the Lord faithfully redirects me back to Him and His Spirit, instead of the things of this world. My goal is to remain in my God-defined situation (my home) and cling to my Lord! When I do that, true refreshment comes that only God can give to me.

Recently, a good friend of mine asked me an interesting question. She asked what I thought it took for a Christian woman to become mature and godly. I thought for a few minutes. I told her that I thought that a Christian woman matures as she releases her heart, interests, and desires from the things of this world. In other words, the less she is entangled in the lures and lusts of this world, the more she transforms into a godly woman. In fact, I've never met a truly mature, godly woman who regularly reads magazines off the newsstands, watches TV nightly, quotes from all the current movies, and wears the most current fashions. The truly godly women that I know have lives that are not preoccupied with these worldly influences. Instead, they are locked and loaded on the Lord Jesus Christ. They have made calculated, strategic choices *not* to engage in the things of this world. Instead, their attention and focus go into pursuing and engaging in their relationship with the Lord. This all reminds me of one of my favorite verses.

Psalm 62:1 My soul finds rest in God alone.

The godly, mature mother experiences a rest that few mothers ever know, but most long for. Plenty of women try to do their mothering without Christ. They go at it, proud and brazen. The end result is guilt, despair, and failure. It will be the same for any of us who don't mother on the Lord's strength. You just can't do enough. You can't be good enough in your own strength. James addresses the end result of when the proud try to live life in their own strength.

> James 4:6b-8a "God opposes the proud but gives grace to the humble." Submit yourselves, then, to God. Resist the devil, and he will flee from you. Come near to God and he will come near to you.

You will fail. The Bible tells us that God will literally oppose you! I'm sure you will agree that no one wants to be in that position before God. Perhaps that is a good thing in the end. In His love, God allows failure and frustration so that we are drawn back to Him.

> Psalm 127:1 Unless the Lord builds the house, its builders labor in vain. Unless the LORD watches over the city, the watchmen stand guard in vain.

In every way, my mothering is an outpouring of my relationship with Christ. Yet it is a heart struggle to keep Christ as the main builder and watchman, while I remain in my rightful position under His headship. Because I always seem to be "in charge" of my children, I can fall into the rut of controlling every situation without any regard to God, or anyone else for that matter. The need for me to be in charge does not legitimize my belligerent attitude to control everyone and everything. Although my motherhood does call for me to be in charge and manage my children's lives, I have to remember that I am under God's authority and need to allow Him to be in charge and to be the main builder of my family. God is in control, not me.

ৡঌৡঌ

The demands of motherhood definitely leave us feeling needy and desperate. The endless, interrupted nights of sleep take their toll. Meeting every single need of little ones causes life to become a complete blur. I remember moments of breaking down in tears and telling Steve, "I don't even know who I am anymore!" I remember those moments of total, emotional numbness.

Meeting the needs of your small children leaves little to no time left for you and getting your needs met. The days turn into months. Twelve months roll around, and you ring in the next New Year with the same weary soul. The truth is that there is never a significant enough break to refresh you for any sustaining duration. It is a challenging season. Thankfully, those moments seem to be mostly in my past now. I think I can tell you, with confidence, that it won't always be that way. But what do you do in that season when things are so challenging, and you feel like you don't even know who you are anymore?

I've rarely met a mother who understands her needs and uses appropriate avenues to meet those needs. I've vacillated in my resolve to handle my own neediness. Interestingly, our neediness can end up masking itself in restlessness. Our restlessness, mixed with times of ambiguity in our vision and purpose, leaves us feeling bored and unfulfilled in our mothering.

We need to deal with our feelings of restlessness and boredom at the heart level, and not by putting a spectacular event or exotic trip on our calendar. There isn't an event in the world that can cure the restless heart of a mother. Mothers do need breaks. Yet there are two kinds of breaks that a mother can take: a break to escape, or a break to refresh.

Go to God

God's Word is the place where a mother can turn to get true strength and renewal. God's Word has sustained me through all of my years of mothering. Reflect on the following four passages with me. Read them carefully. There are truths in these verses that I have held on to for years. I have returned, again and again to these same verses. And every single time, they have ministered to my soul. The Word is richer and deeper than any of us will ever experience in a lifetime.

> *2 Chronicles 7:14 "If my people, who are called by my name, will humble themselves and pray and seek my face and turn from their wicked ways, then will I hear from heaven and will forgive their sin and will heal their land."*

> *2 Chronicles 16:9 "For the eyes of the LORD range throughout the earth to strengthen those whose hearts are fully committed to him."*

Jeremiah 29:13 "You will seek me and find me when you seek me with all your heart."

You get the idea, don't you? Every single word of these verses has been my food. They have been my comfort. More than anything, they have worked for me! In the same way, I am confident that God's Word will work for you too! The very best thing that we have to offer our children, and our husbands, is our own personal, vibrant, growing relationship with the Lord. In the same way, the very best thing that we have to offer *ourselves* is a personal, vibrant, growing relationship with the Lord.

ملانه‏

Isaiah 58:10-11 "And if you spend yourselves in behalf of the hungry and satisfy the needs of the oppressed, then your light will rise in the darkness, and your night will become like the noonday. The LORD will guide you always; he will satisfy your needs in a sun-scorched land and will strengthen your frame. You will be like a well-watered garden, like a spring whose waters never fail."

We all spend ourselves one way or another. If we look around, we can see the vast possibilities of how a person can spend themselves.

When I found this verse, I actually sat down and laughed. I am not sure if God meant to humor me, but I thought it was hilarious. God said you can spend yourself on behalf of the hungry, which described my life to a tee. You see, I had certain children that had developed this demanding habit called eating. They really liked eating, and they liked eating all of the time!

One of my little boys had a routine with his habit. He would sit down with the family and eat a decent meal. After he finished, I would take him to the bathroom to clean his hands and face. Then, I would scoot him off to go play. He would do one lap around the house, promptly walk back into the kitchen, and say, "I hun-gwy, Mama." Do you remember the voice of Rolly, the hungry little puppy, in "101 Dalmatians", when he would always beg his mama for food? That was what it was like for me as I looked down into my little boy's eyes and heard his familiar request for more food.

It always made me chuckle when he would announce that he was hungry after being gone from the dinner table less than five minutes. But the adorable part was that when I chuckled, he would furrow his little eyebrows and, in a slightly growly voice, say, "I weely am, Mama. I hun-gwy!" He didn't see the humor in it one bit, which made it even funnier to me. After ruffling his hair, I would scoop him up in my arms, buckle him back into his highchair, and go find "round two" of dinner.

It's been a lot of work keeping my gang fed. Considering all of the trips to the grocery store, the hours preparing and cleaning up after meals, and the hours getting out and cleaning up after snack time, I think it is safe to say that I have spent myself on behalf of the hungry.

This verse tells me that if I spend myself in a certain way, God promises to do amazing things. He says that He will strengthen my frame. He says that He will satisfy my needs. He says that He will make me like a spring whose waters never fail! Wow, do I feel like I need that or what?

I'll take it. It makes all of those hours of preparing meals and all of those trips to the grocery store well worth it!

ஒ௭ஒ௭

The Truth Project

If you are like me, you have a default thought-life that is based on self-centeredness. We run the same continual stream of thoughts through our heads. These thoughts keep us tethered to our self-centeredness. We frequently catch ourselves thinking: *It's all about me, how I feel, and how I want things to go.* This type of thought life leaves us feeling trapped and struggling to stay encouraged.

One of the greatest revelations that I ever had was when I heard Rick Whitney, a pastor and father of seven, say, "It is your job to keep yourself encouraged!" That rocked my world. I must be honest; I thought it was Steve's job. Steve felt quite liberated when I took ownership of my own encouragement.

We need to set ourselves on a course to change our thought life from an emotion-based thought life, to a truth-based thought life! A truth-based thought life ultimately results in a truth-based heart. Even though I stole the name from Focus on the Family, I see my life as my own personal "Truth Project."

Teaching my children to transfer truth to their thinking is one of my main goals for my kids as well. If you don't believe me, just ask them! They would probably roll their eyes, smile, and confirm that I am committed to that happening in our home. I want them to view their lives as their own personal "Truth Project." As a mother, that is one of the main things that I choose to focus on; I just happen to do all of the laundry and cooking along the way. When the Lord captures my heart with one of His truths, I feel freedom! And that drives me to have my kids experience that freedom also. The more I connect and understand God's truths, the more I sense His freedom and deliverance.

I cannot overemphasize the importance of connecting our souls to truth. All the while, we must continue to do all that is required of us as mothers. When my children were little ones, it was often very difficult to get consistent, uninterrupted time in the Word. In the early years, I spent way too much time being frustrated and discouraged by my children interrupting my time with the Lord. In God's grace, He led me down a path that has brought great freedom and liberty. That freedom came through memorizing His Word…slowly, methodically, and daily. Basically, I became a memorization junkie as I carried my babies around on my hip. Since those early days, I've never stopped! I am completely convinced that memorizing, focusing on one verse at a time, is what sustained me through those crazy days.

I literally memorized hundreds of verses during my early days of motherhood. I had to! I just couldn't seem to have a meaningful "quiet time," no matter how hard I tried. To me, a "quiet time" meant that I was actually supposed to be refreshed at the end of the time, and felt that I had connected to God. That just didn't seem to happen very often. As my dear friend put it, "A mother's quiet times can easily become just a training time." And that is so true. By the time that you get everyone in their right places, redirect the children as they get distracted, and help the baby hold her Precious Moments Bible right side up, quiet times are often over, and it's time for breakfast!

After so many frustrating attempts, God helped me come up with my own style of "quiet times." I would write some good verses in a spiral index-card pack. I would then place that card pack on my kitchen counter, and flip it open to any verse. It didn't really matter which verse. Trust me; I was desperate enough that anything in God's Word helped, soothed, and encouraged me. Eventually, I trained myself to focus and meditate on just one verse at a time. I would soak on one verse for a couple of hours. Later, as I walked through the kitchen, I would flip the page to a new verse and start the process all over again.

Over time, that method of meditating on one verse at a time became a legitimate, effective form of "quiet times" for me. To this day, I still frequently do that as a quiet time. Sometimes, even after I am able to sit with the Lord and have time with Him, I can still feel like my soul needs more. You know how sometimes nothing seems to stick? What's a mother supposed to do? Often, she just keeps plugging away with her spiritual tank on "empty." I eventually learned to follow up my regular quiet times with meditating on a verse out of one of my packs of verses. Around my home, we even tagged a name to my packs of verses. We call them "truth packs!"

I've made truth packs concentrating on different areas in my life. For example, I have made truth packs on marriage enrichment, disciplining children, biblical speech, etc. By the way, I have even started implementing these into my children's lives too. My oldest five kids all have truth packs that they regularly read through. One kid might have a truth pack dealing with pride. Another one might be working through a truth pack dealing with identity. A different child might be developing a truth pack dealing with telling the truth. We usually direct them to collect verses on an area that they are currently struggling with or interested in.

I want to train my children to view their truth packs as an effective way of spending time with God. I want them to feel the freedom to be creative and connect with the Lord as the Spirit leads, not feeling obligated to "stick to the program"! Life often does run at such a crazy pace that mothers can't, or don't, have effective quiet times. Then they feel guilty! I don't want my kiddos to get in that rut when the busyness of life hits them and they lose their spiritual footing! Truth packs have been amazingly effective for my children and me for years now!

A Storehouse

I once heard a godly mother explain how our hearts are like storehouses. She described how we all make choices of what things we store up in our hearts. I will always remember that. I like to think of my heart that way. I regularly remind myself that I am making deposits in my storehouse. My truth packs accomplish that.

So, why is that important? Well, I have experienced amazing moments when God has stirred up some truth from my storehouse to keep me going, redirect me, or encourage me. This is often right in the middle of the craziness of mothering my kids! Because those truths were deposited into my storehouse, God could just bring them to my mind right on the spot. I didn't have to go find my Bible to hear from the Lord. Over the years, those moments have helped me keep a close and meaningful relationship with the Lord.

Focus

Distraction can be a mother's worst enemy. The term, "multi-tasking," seems to downplay the demands of a mother. Come up with the word that describes multi-tasking to the nth degree and *that* is motherhood. One duty calls for our attention, thereby pulling our attention from something else that also needs our attention. Exasperated, we can feel like there just isn't enough of us to go around.

For this very reason, a mother needs to carefully prioritize her life. First of all, she must determine exactly what she is striving toward. From years of experience, I would encourage you to consider letting go of the goal to have a balanced life. It seems almost scandalous to suggest that, doesn't it? For years, I thought we were supposed to strive to live balanced lives. I saw the Christian world advocate this idea of bringing balance to one's life. There seemed to be a universal, overall acceptance of the idea that it is unhealthy and ill-advised to live "unbalanced." I even thought that a balanced life was a part of "God's will" for my life.

In the realm of mothering, I thought that I would actually be a better mom if I kept my life balanced! I tried to unite the pursuit of a balanced life with the demands of motherhood. What was the result? I was left even more self-focused and frustrated in my mothering. Incidentally, being self-focused and frustrated are most unhelpful on a day-to-day basis, especially when you are tending to self-focused children! Now, I firmly believe the idea that the believer should have a balanced life is complete rubbish!

> *Luke 9:23-25 Then he said to them all: "If anyone would come after me, he must deny himself and take up his cross daily and follow me. For whoever wants to save his life will lose it, but whoever loses his life for me will save it. What good is it for a man to gain the whole world, and yet lose or forfeit his very self?"*

I just don't see the pursuit of a "balanced life" supported in the Scriptures. I mean, how do you "lay down your life" and stay balanced? How does a mother "deny" herself and maintain a balanced life? How does a mother "lose her life" and stay balanced? It seems to me that the biblical command to lose your life for Christ's sake is the opposite of having a balanced life. When I think of the word, "balance," I think of things being equally distributed or weighted. The Scriptures actually seem to encourage me to live an unbalanced, sold-out life!

When a mother desperately tries to balance it all, she ends up not doing anything well. The world applauds her for seemingly being able to do it all. Everyone asks her, "How do you do it all?" She smiles broadly, but her children don't. They are tired. They are tired of being dragged around town while Mommy "performs" for everyone else!

Proverbs 14:1 The wise woman builds her house, but with her own hands the foolish one tears hers down.

The foolish mother tears her own house down by working to *include* God's agenda into her agenda. My agenda is usually self-seeking; God's agenda is selfless and altruistic. Since they are opposing agendas, trying to combine the two usually doesn't go smoothly.

Proverbs 23:4 Do not wear yourself out to get rich; have the wisdom to show restraint.

The Bible tells us that it takes wisdom to show restraint. The wise woman shows restraint as she carefully builds her house. She is not given to the pulls of our society. Unfortunately, the Christian community has been lulled into the world's thinking. We are scared to say "no" to anything that is asked of us. We are also afraid of not having our kids involved in every activity under the sun. We are afraid to say "no" because we don't want our kids to miss out on any "opportunities." Perhaps, we weren't able to do all of the activities that we wanted to when we were children. Or, perhaps, we feel like we owe these activities to our children.

Either way, these activities are eating away at your family's time together. These activities are sucking away your energy by making you so tired from running around all day, every day! They are interfering with having any meaningful conversation or relationship with your kids. The truth is that your schedule doesn't allow for it! Your schedule is too packed full of activities to allow for adequate family time and God-time.

The hectic, activity-driven lifestyle leaves many mothers with regrets. They wish they had quieted their lives down to focus on the important things that needed to happen in their homes. It takes wisdom to say "no" to all of the endless possibilities, while saying "yes" to a lifestyle that narrowly focuses our time on the essential things! Even more so, it takes daily self-control and an undistracted mother with a vision. Our vision has to drive our schedules, not our activities!

≪≫≪≫

I have some confessions to make. For some of you, they might be refreshing and encouraging. For the rest of you, you are probably going to feel disappointed and let down by me. Here it goes: I am, and always have been, a terrible cook. My family eats way too many processed foods. I don't drink even half of the amount of water that I am supposed to everyday. I don't even own a fancy water bottle. Any exercise program that I have started in the last eighteen years has fizzled out with neglect and interrupting circumstances. I don't wear the latest fashions, although I confess to sometimes trying to. I nap almost every day and have for the past eighteen years. I have dried Cheerios smashed on the seats of my van at all times. I only clean out my car if I know you are going to be riding with me, and even then I might not get around to it. I rarely send a timely birthday card, or *any* card for that matter, to my closest friends. I confess to always signing up for the easiest food items to bring to church events. There are Legos, Polly Pockets, and assorted naked dollies strewn all over the playroom floor on most days. I have never once rotated the kids' toys in eighteen years, although I always thought it was a great idea. I have never completed one single photo album of our lives in over twenty years. Even our wedding pictures aren't in an album yet. I have never repainted a room in my house. Nothing hangs on the walls in my house that has cost us more than ten dollars.

I could keep going, but you get the idea. I must admit that when I write out that list, my heart does sink a little bit. I am tempted to feel like a failure. I find myself thinking that, surely, I could do a better job at some of those things. Am I just being lazy? Perhaps. Or is it possible that most of those things on the list have been intentionally bumped from my list of priorities?

Let me tell you a little secret. Those things are part of our elimination plan. They are things that Steve and I have sacrificed because we are busy with many important things, and we can't do it all. We have let some things go, even worthy things, so we could do more important things–like raising our children.

Eliminate

Nehemiah 6:1-4 When word came to Sanballat, Tobiah, Geshem the Arab and the rest of our enemies that I had rebuilt the wall and not a gap was left in it—though up to that time I had not set the doors in the gates— Sanballat and Geshem sent me this message: "Come, let us meet together in one of the villages on the plain of Ono." But they were scheming to harm me; so I sent messengers to them with this reply: "I am carrying on a great project and cannot go down. Why should the work stop while I leave it and go down to you?" Four times they sent me the same message, and each time I gave them the same answer.

Nehemiah was a wise man. He knew what was most important. He knew what to eliminate. I'm sure he felt the peer pressure. He might have even worried about what they would think of him. He might have feared retaliation. But he stood his ground. Nehemiah's words run through my head when my phone rings. Someone from the "outside world" might call, asking me to get together or commit to one thing or another. Well, the same truth holds for me, as it held for Nehemiah. I truly am carrying on a great project. I have to ask myself if I can really afford to take time away from raising my children. As we prioritize raising our children, it calls us to eliminate other things. I do say 'yes' to all kinds of other commitments, but only after Steve and I carefully weigh them against *all* of our priorities. Honestly, I've had to say no to "important" things—more than I have been comfortable with. Yet, as I reflect back, I am so thankful that I did. Every single thing that I was able to eliminate allowed me more freedom to mother without distractions.

You can't have it all! You can die trying; I've seen mothers with that kind of stubborn attitude. Personally, I just want to encourage you with my own testimony. Perhaps it will give you the courage and faith to follow Christ in what He is personally calling you to give up.

For me, that has meant that I gave up all of my hobbies. Honestly, I didn't have any amazing hobbies to begin with. Maybe that helped me in this step of obedience. But it was still hard to not be able to dabble in some things that I might enjoy. I just can't fit them in anymore.

I guess there was one thing I gave up that I did cherish. That was my daily walks. That was probably the hardest thing I gave up. (Actually, it's a toss-up between my walks and my sleep, but I had no choice with my sleep!) Before I had children, I had developed the habit of walking, praying, and memorizing for about an hour a day. As a wife without children, that worked beautifully. Needless to say, I fell in love with that privilege. When I was a young mother, Steve and I fought about that one "privilege" more than a few times. What it came down to was that we just didn't have the resources to make that happen anymore on a consistent, daily basis. Maybe I would be able to go for a walk here or there, but not consistently. That was tough for me. Yet, in God's grace, I relented. And God proved to be enough, even in that!

৵৬৵৬

My house plants also had to go. Okay, that one wasn't so tough. I guess you could say I gave them up out of disgust! I had several young children at the time. One day, I was walking around my house noticing all of my pathetic plants that I had repeatedly neglected for years because I was busy with the children. At least, that was my justification for the condition of my plants. Now, some of you might be talented enough to do both–water your plants and mother–but, for me, that seemed to be a challenging endeavor! That day, I got a large garbage bag and I put them all out of their misery. That happened many years ago and I haven't had a single plant in my house since then. Sometimes, I long for a plant. Then, I remind myself: There will be a season for that in my future, but not right now. So I wait for that day. One of these days, I am going to go to the store and pick out some pretty little plants to enjoy in my house. But not now. I need to stay focused and attentive to the task at hand, which is raising the disciples that the Lord has given me. In a future season, I will grow plants. For now, I am growing children.

Does that sound extreme? God has called me to give up my life for Him. If giving up a few plants will help me have a little more time and be a little more focused, then doing so seems like the easiest of sacrifices.

෧෨෧෨෧

Boundaries

The process of elimination is your ally. So is the process of implementing boundaries. Consider it well worth your time to place certain boundaries in your daily routine. Boundaries on your schedule and activities allow you to spend good, quality time busy in your home, mothering your children. For example, think through your time on the internet. Can you put some kind of a boundary on that area of your life? Maybe you could check your email and your facebook after you get the kids to bed at night, or during naptime. I am always amazed at how much time actually slips away when I think I just sat at the computer for five minutes! Those things definitely warrant boundaries. Think through your time on the phone. Can you put some kind of a boundary on that area of your life? Setting boundaries in these areas has been a blessing in my own life and has freed me up to give my attention to my children.

୧୨ଚ୧୨ଚ

One boundary that Steve and I established years ago was that I wouldn't answer the phone before noon on a daily basis. Even now, sometimes I will get unfocused and answer the phone before noon. Then, the Lord will gently remind me of what a blessing that boundary has been in my life. As a response to the Lord's nudging, I will recommit to keeping that boundary.

You might ask, "Kathleen, what is the big deal with not answering the phone before noon every day?" The fruit of giving my full attention to my children every morning has been tremendous for both them and me. The children are so much more peaceful and obedient if I am faithful and consistent to give them my full attention every morning. As long as I carve out the whole morning to just engage with them, they typically will be peaceful for the rest of the day. And what benefit is it for me? I get the bonus of not feeling guilty about being a distracted mother. After years of mothering, I value that freedom from guilt very highly.

୧୨ଚ୧୨ଚ

1 Thessalonians 5:21 Test everything. Hold on to the good.

Every area of your life–housecleaning, television, movie watching, to-do lists, daily agendas, hobbies, etc.— warrants careful examination. Remember that you are trying to establish a daily environment that frees you up to be the mother that God has called you to be. Don't you agree that is worth careful consideration? I regularly revisit my goal to mother without distractions.

Admittedly, I usually get irritated when someone suggests that I should examine my life. First, I seem to have no time to give attention to such heady things. Second, I seem to have lost my ability to concentrate on any one thing long enough to draw any conclusions. And, third, someone in my house is going to interrupt me during my self-examination exercise. Yes, I understand your deep desire to throw this book out the window at the suggestion of examining every area of your life. I know how impossible it all seems. But, let me encourage you with what I have experienced over the years. Although it probably seems impossible to successfully self-reflect on *anything*, let alone *every area* of your life, the Lord has been faithful. He has revealed the very things that He wants me to change, focus on, or modify in my mothering. I don't have to find a quiet room, muster up all of my concentration, and keep my kids from interrupting me in order for the Lord to lead and direct me. I just need to come to Him with a willing and yielded heart. He has led me in my spirit as I have stood in my kitchen making peanut butter and jelly sandwiches for lunch. He can do the same for you; all you have to do is present your willing heart before Him. You will be amazed at how effective your "self-examination" times can go in the midst of you faithfully mothering.

Do the Next Right Thing

Eventually everything got overwhelming and complicated. With so many little ones needing my attention all of the time, I became flustered at the amount of work left at the end of each day. The incredible number of small decisions that I needed to make to keep everyone's lives moving forward became crushing. I felt like I got stuck on the simplest of decisions—what to say *yes* to and what to say *no* to. How was I supposed to get it all done? What exactly should I prioritize with my time?

So the Lord simplified it for me! He said, *do the next right thing*. It worked for me in every way. (Incidentally, it works for me directing my children too.) That little saying may not seem powerful when you read it on the page, but try using it tomorrow and see if it cultivates direction and clarity in your mothering. Now, when I sense that overwhelming "stuck" feeling, I will just whisper to myself, *Kathleen, just do the next right thing. Come on, girl, you can do it. Just do the next right thing.* It is surprising how that helps me push through those bewildering moments and keep everything, and everyone, moving forward.

2 Thessalonians 3:13b Never tire of doing what is right.

The Lord will lead you in sorting it out and knowing what to do with it all. But, in the meantime, your family needs you to keep pressing on. Just do the next right thing and pray that God will give you definition in how to get everything done.

❧❧❧❧

A Mother in Progress

Your kids don't need you to be perfect in all of this. They aren't perfect either. Keep reminding yourself that the most important thing you can give your kids is someone to imitate. They get to watch their mother pursue God. And what is the beauty of it all? God is completely sufficient to get each one of us through this entire process.

Isaiah 30:21 Whether you turn to the right or to the left, your ears will hear a voice behind you, saying, "This is the way; walk in it."

Isaiah 41:10 "So do not fear, for I am with you; do not be dismayed, for I am your God. I will strengthen you and help you; I will uphold you with my righteous right hand."

Aren't those verses comforting? God is directing us as we move forward. And He is moving forward with us. He's right there, helping and strengthening us. Those truths should be anchors that steady our faith as we do the next right thing.

❧❧❧❧

Hebrews 12:2-3 Let us fix our eyes on Jesus, the author and perfecter of our faith, who for the joy set before him endured the cross, scorning its shame, and sat down at the right hand of the throne of God. Consider him who endured such opposition from sinful men, so that you will not grow weary and lose heart.

I need to spend my "heart energy" on fixing my eyes on Jesus. How much clearer could the Word be? When I struggle with losing heart as a mother, here is the answer for me to engage in! Fix my eyes on Jesus. I can do that. That is a clear enough instruction to obey right in the moment. In order to focus on Jesus, I funnel all of my thoughts toward that one goal, purging any thoughts that divert my attention. Try to do that! It is harder than it seems. When I work on this exercise, I am always amazed at how much of my thinking has nothing to do with Jesus! It has taken intense training on my part for me to insert Jesus into my everyday thought life. And I still don't feel like I have mastered it by any means.

> *1 Timothy 4:7-8 Have nothing to do with godless myths and old wives' tales; rather, train yourself to be godly. For physical training is of some value, but godliness has value for all things, holding promise for both the present life and the life to come.*
>
> *2 Corinthians 10:5 We demolish arguments and every pretension that sets itself up against the knowledge of God, and we take captive every thought to make it obedient to Christ.*

It is easy to just try to survive. However, we need to aspire to more than just survival. We can actually grow into godly women right in the midst of the chaos of raising our children

You can't give your kids a perfect mother. You can't even offer them a mother who tried her hardest. You and I both know that there were days that we hardly tried at all. When I reflect on all of the times that I spoke too harshly, emotionally pushed them away because I was tired, and engaged with them about their behavior and not their heart, I can get a sinking feeling in my stomach. It is discouraging to think that all we have to offer our kids is a mother who has made enough mistakes to scar any child's life. No amount of fun birthday parties, yummy meals, and trips to the park could possibly make up for some of my mistakes as a mother.

That is a pretty despairing thought, isn't it? What can possibly cover the mistakes that we have made with our children? There is only one right answer: forgiveness. Remember that *you* need to connect to Christ and His forgiveness. In the same way, you need to connect *your children* to Christ and His forgiveness. If the only one they are connected to is you, then you've given them a defective and faulty source of identity and hope.

2 Corinthians 5:20 We are therefore Christ's ambassadors, as though God were making his appeal through us. We implore you on Christ's behalf: Be reconciled to God.

God wants to use you, as an ambassador, to draw your kids to Himself. Your identity is based on what God thinks of you. Your children also need to be taught that their identity is based on what God thinks of them. Their identity has to be developed beyond what you, your husband, and others think of them. You need to connect them to God in the most thorough and fundamental way possible. Only then can your children receive and embrace your love and, at the same time, not be scarred by your mistakes in mothering. Only when your children embrace their own need for forgiveness, can they begin to forgive others, including you. That is one of the beautiful benefits of pointing them to Christ—for their sake and for your sake! In the end, you both need to be connected to Christ, His forgiveness, and His perfect love.

In other words, your children must see that you understand your forgiveness, that you are connected to God, and that you are growing in Him. Melody Green, the wife of the late musician Keith Green, wrote:

> *The hardest testing ground for our Christianity is right in our own homes—with our parents, our brothers and sisters, our husbands and wives, and our children. If we can't prove our Christianity there, we can't prove it anywhere.*

You must to prove to your kids that following Christ works and that He can be trusted. Your kids need to be front row spectators to the work of the Spirit in your souls. A changing life is more powerful than any conversation that you can have with your kids.

1 Timothy 4:12b-16 Set an example for the believers in speech, in life, in love, in faith and in purity...Be diligent in these matters; give yourself wholly to them, so that everyone may see your progress. Watch your life and

doctrine closely. Persevere in them, because if you do, you will save both yourself and your hearers.

The Word calls us as Christians to set an example for others. What, specifically, are we supposed to set an example in? Well, the list starts off with a biggie — in speech. That first directive is a lifelong pursuit for all of us!

The list continues: in life, in love, in faith, and in purity. Okay, God is describing the mom that I want to be, but it is only going to happen by the power of His Spirit working in me! My response to the first part of the passage is often discouragement. I can hide my head and think that I am never going to set a good enough example in those areas! I can feel like I could never be that for my kids. Then, I read on and apply verses fifteen and sixteen to my life, and I find so much hope. The Word says to me, *Kathleen, be diligent in these matters and give yourself wholly to them, so that everyone may see your progress!* There is my hope! My hope is in my kids seeing my progress! I sure can't give my kids a perfect mom, but I can give my kids a mom who is growing in "these matters." Those aspiring directives are encouraging to me. I can do those things–in Christ.

God, in His loving grace, then gives you and me that ultimate hope! He tells us to persevere in the things that He listed. And why should you and I persevere in them? Verse sixteen says, "Because, if you do, you will save both yourself and your hearers!" Amazing! Who are my hearers? My precious children! This is one of those verses that, when I read it, I just want to throw my whole life at it because of the payoff! Take Him at His word. Throw your whole life on every word He says in the Scriptures. When He says we can save our hearers, we should believe Him!

132

Think about this with me; what would the fruit of giving yourself wholly to those things look like? Definitely everyone would see progress in your life! I also envision rich fruit in your children's souls. Your choices can bring life and peace to your family, your home, and your own soul. Elisabeth Elliott, one of my all-time favorite Christian authors, said:

God never issued instructions which He is not prepared to enable us to follow. The contrast between the actual and the ideal, between the reality and the holy standard, is bridged by the grace of God, and by our prayers for the application of that grace.

Fellow mothers, we are forgiven. The Lord explains the breadth of His mercy:

Psalm 103:12 As far as the east is from the west, so far has he removed our transgressions from us.

We are washed clean. We stand before our Lord clothed in righteousness. People try connecting their righteousness with their deeds and their performance, instead of God. I see mothers who think their righteousness comes from their healthy living choices, like drinking bottled water and only eating whole grains! Those things *can* be fine, but may we never be mothers who mask our pride in a self-righteous lifestyle. If you choose to define your righteousness through your own list of "*dos* and *don'ts*" in your lifestyle, you are left to include every single one of your failures too.

133

And the worst part is that you will also teach your children to define their righteousness according to their behavior. That is a grave mistake—far bigger than any yelling episode you could ever have with your child. Our kids need to learn to separate their righteousness from their behavior and define it through Christ's sacrifice on the cross. And so do we.

A great litmus test to examine if something in our lives is truly biblical righteousness (or if it is just self-righteousness) is this question: "Does it point an observer to the cross?" If not, it is a form of self-righteousness. It might be admirable, but it is not legitimate righteousness. Jesus' sacrifice on the cross is the payment that we can claim. From that sacrifice, we are clothed in a righteousness that is not reliant on our actions. God's strength and grace is the well that we have to draw from for our perseverance. In all of this, we are talking about our daily obedience to the Lord. It is our daily choices that cause us to grow in Christ.

෴෴

An Imperfect Mother

Years ago, I remember that I went downstairs to get something and noticed that the children had left all of the CDs scattered on the floor around the computer. Annoyed, I called all of the children to the scene. I then proceeded to give them a good, strong lecture about keeping things picked up, valuing the things God had given us, and living respectfully with others. The children listened with hung heads. When I finished my spiel, they quickly scrambled to pick up the mess.

Still annoyed, I climbed back up the stairs to go about my business. As I rounded the corner, I stumbled over something on the floor. Irritated, I looked down to see my own shoes. I pushed them aside with my foot and went on into the kitchen. As I walked over to the table, I kicked something under it. I peered under the table to see what it was. I saw another pair of my shoes that I had left there the day before. As I picked up the shoes to put them away, I rounded the corner and noticed a third pair of my shoes thrown in the foyer!

I smiled to myself. Quietly, I retraced my steps to the table and tossed my shoes back under the table. Then, I went to the top of the stairs. In the same annoyed voice that I had used with the children, I called them upstairs. They all came, heads still hanging low. They were bracing themselves for round two of this lecture. When they got to the top of the stairs, I annoyingly asked them, "Whose shoes are those?"

Their eyes followed my pointed finger to the floor. One of them meekly offered, "Yours?"

I said, "That's right! Follow me!" Continuing in my annoyed voice, I asked, "And whose shoes are those under the table?"

The kids looked under the table. Their faces came back up. With big, cautious smiles, they answered, "Yours?"

I said, "That's right! Follow me!" I marched my little brigade to the foyer. By this time the mood had changed and the children were starting to quietly giggle with twinkles in their eyes. I pointed to my shoes laying in the foyer. With a weary and slightly defeated voice, I slowly said, "And whose shoes are those?"

With no hesitation and big smiles, they gleefully shouted in unison, "Yours!"

I sat down and said, "That's right, guys. Those are all my shoes that I have left thrown all over the house! Mommy also needs to learn to pick up her stuff, value the things God has given her, and live respectfully with others."

The children broke into laughter and threw their arms around me, saying, "Oh, that's okay, Mommy. We still love you!"

As they joyfully ran off to finish picking up their mess, I yelled after them, "We're all still going to grow in this area. You guys just wait and see. Mommy's going to change and keep her stuff picked up from now on!" (Steve wants me to assure all of you readers that I still have room to grow in this area.)

> *Jeremiah 9:24 "But if people want to brag, let them brag that they understand and know me. Let them brag that I am the* LORD, *and that I am kind and fair, and that I do things that are right on earth. This kind of bragging pleases me," says the Lord. (NCV)*

I can't give my children a perfect mother, but I can give them a mother who is peaceful before the Lord. I can even give them a mother who brags. No, she doesn't brag about herself. Instead, she brags about her Lord and His amazing transforming power in her life!

Years ago, I found a picture in *Life Magazine*. I cut it out and tucked it in my Bible. It has been there ever since that day. The picture is a reminder of the woman I want to become. The picture shows a very old lady sitting on a metal folding chair. The caption states that she is in a temporary emergency shelter after her town was hit by an earthquake. This dear old woman is peacefully reading her *Santa Biblia* as the world around her is in complete chaos. She has a tattered wool skirt that hangs down just above her ankles. She is wearing, what looks like, some much-worn Teva sandals with wool socks. She seems cozy in her oversized, grey sweatshirt. A wool shawl is loosely wrapped around her head and over her shoulders as her white hair peeks out from underneath. Her hands and face expose the many years of a long-lived life.

In my opinion, she is completely beautiful in every way. Perhaps no one in the whole world would pick this old woman out as the beautiful woman they want to grow into—except me. I have announced to my whole family that this is the woman who I want to grow into as I age. And I am serious. I want to grow into this woman in every way—down to her wool socks and Tevas. I need to go out and buy myself a pair of those sandals because it is going to take several years of wearing them to get them to look as worn as hers!

Her face and her actions say it all. She knows to Whom she belongs and in Whom she trusts. She is still making that choice to read her Spanish Bible as she continues to seek God after so many years of life. The peace that is evident in her posture and face is priceless. I want to experience that in my old age.

Isaiah 46:4 Even to your old age and gray hairs I am he, I am he who will sustain you. I have made you and I will carry you; I will sustain you and I will rescue you.

Those are powerful words and they so aptly fit the little old lady's relationship with the Lord! This dear soul is being rescued, in her own way, in the midst of an earthquake. From the picture, I imagine that if someone in that shelter approached her, she would tell them of her faith in the Lord. I am driven to her Confidence. I want to model that old woman for my children and for my grandchildren!

Several years ago, someone close to us died. We were talking with the children about all of the things that you talk about when someone dies. The conversation touched on what would become of all of that person's possessions. We told the kids that they would be distributed out to her family and friends. My son, Silas, around ten years old at the time, spoke up and said, "I know what I want when Mom dies." All of the rest of us were a little startled with his comment.

Eventually someone recovered enough to ask, "What?" He said, "I want that picture of that old lady she keeps in her Bible, the one of the woman she wants to become when she gets old!" It was adorable that my son knew how important that picture was to me and wanted it when I died.

Proverbs 31:25-31 She is clothed with strength and dignity; she can laugh at the days to come. She speaks with wisdom, and faithful instruction is on her tongue. She watches over the affairs of her household and does not eat the bread of idleness. Her children arise and call her blessed; her husband also, and he praises her: "Many women do noble things, but you surpass them all." Charm is deceptive, and beauty is fleeting; but a woman who fears the LORD is to be praised. Give her the reward she has earned, and let her works bring her praise at the city gate.

Becoming this Proverbs 31 woman is a lifelong pursuit for me. I see a mother who is bringing wisdom and faithful instruction to her children, and loving her husband. She is committed to managing her home. And most importantly, she fears the Lord. I want to receive the same reward that she has earned. But, mothers, she had to earn it first. And the same is true for you and for me. We have to earn that reward and praise.

Conclusion

Know this; God is sufficient for all of your mothering. If God gave you your children, you can know that He gave you the tools, resources, wisdom, godly counsel, and everything else that is necessary to raise them for His glory. This is true for each one of us! What a stabilizing hope for all of us!

Of course, it isn't enough to just believe this. We must also act on it. What is our part in this? We have to set ourselves on a daily course of pursuing Him, obeying His Word, and believing truths, instead of our fears, insecurities, and wrong thinking. We have to be determined. A sporadic, intermittent course, where we turn to God only when we are desperate and at the end of our tether, is not likely to adequately prepare us for the trials of this journey. A consistent, daily course of following Him is fundamental for us to make it. There is much hope in that course of action!

࿐࿐࿐

Of course, I am not done raising my children. I still have lots of work left to do. My youngest child is just three years old! I know that it will be sixteen more years before our house will sit empty of children. I pray often that the Lord will continue to give me the strength and perseverance to raise every single one of them as He would want.

࿐࿐࿐

Isaiah 50:7 Because the Sovereign LORD helps me, I will not be disgraced. Therefore have I set my face like flint, and I know I will not be put to shame.

Flint is a very hard rock. It represents guts and determination. Where does that kind of determination come from? It comes from knowing that, in the end, God will make everything right, and I will not be ashamed. It's going to take exactly that kind of attitude for me to finish this journey of motherhood and raise my youngest son to become a godly man! On one hand, I tremble at the long road ahead of me. Yet God has proven Himself faithful to me. So, on the other hand, I press on, taking it one day at a time, knowing that God is walking every step of this with me.

Psalm 119:112 My heart is set on keeping your decrees to the very end.

Years ago, I memorized this simple verse. I had seen many mothers start out strong, only to lose steam and become derailed somewhere along the way. In God's grace, I will be a woman that keeps God's decrees to the very end.

Judges 5:21 "March on, my soul, be strong."

As I was skimming the Scriptures, my eye caught these little words buried in the middle of a completely different biblical thought. What a battle cry for my soul! I can totally relate to those marching orders for my mothering journey. It is my soul that needs to march on and persevere more than anything else.

ৡৣৡৣ

Walk in faith. Faith is important. It's the only thing that counts in the end. Remember that your faith is what will please God when it is all said and done. It's amazing to know that God is not necessarily concerned with whether we do everything right or wrong; instead, He only measures it according to our faith.

Galatians 5:6b The only thing that counts is faith expressing itself through love.

Hebrews 11:6 And without faith it is impossible to please God, because anyone who comes to him must believe that he exists and that he rewards those who earnestly seek him.

The things that I am most confident about in this book are all of the verses that are listed. Every thought of mine risks error—error in misinterpretation, error in under emphasis, error in overemphasis, or error in application. However, I am sure of God's Word. It is completely sound in its advice. It has the perfect measure of emphasis and it is flawless in its application. Cling to Him. If you lay this book down and never pick it up again, but choose to pick up your Bible and faithfully study it for the rest of your life, I will be most pleased and feel like God has answered my prayers. It is truly all about your personal relationship with Christ, as you walk hand in hand with Him.

I am going to sign off and head downstairs to see if I can fold the clothes before they get wrinkly. I know that mothering can seem exhausting and hopeless. I hope the lessons that God has taught me will resonate with you and strengthen you. May God get all the glory from your motherhood. Walk in faith. I pray that you are blessed and highly favored as you pursue your Savior and His calling.

Appendix

Verse Index

Old Testament	Page
Deuteronomy 6:4-9	90
Deuteronomy 7:9	78
Judges 5:21	141
2 Chronicles 16:9	110
2 Chronicles 7:14	110
Nehemiah 6:1-4	121
Psalm 62:1	107
Psalm 103:12	133
Psalm 119:112	141
Psalm 127:1	108
Psalm 127:3	40
Psalm 144:12	41
Proverbs 4:23	29
Proverbs 14:1	119
Proverbs 22:15	93
Proverbs 23:4	119
Proverbs 23:26	56
Proverbs 29:15	93
Proverbs 31:25-31	138
Ecclesiastes 3:1	29
Isaiah 30:21	128
Isaiah 41:10	128
Isaiah 43:19	67
Isaiah 50:7	140
Isaiah 58:10-11	111
Isaiah 46:4	138
Jeremiah 9:24	136
Jeremiah 18:1-7	46
Jeremiah 29:13	111
Jonah 2:8	105
Habakkuk 1:13	25

New Testament	Page
Matthew 6:19-21	95
Matthew 6:33	71,91
Matthew 12:34	29
Mark 12:30	61
Luke 9:23-25	118
John 12:24	58
John 15:16-17	82
John 21:21-22	61
Romans 3:23	25
Romans 5:8	26
Romans 6:23	25
Romans 8:6	88
Romans 12:1	62
Romans 12:2	92
1 Corinthians 4:2	59
1 Corinthians 15:58	60
2 Corinthians 3:2-3	48
2 Corinthians 5:20	130
2 Corinthians 9:6-7	63
2 Corinthians 10:5	129
Galatians 5:6	141
Galatians 5:22-23a	88
Galatians 6:7	31
Galatians 6:9	33
Ephesians 4:29	85
Ephesians 5:1-2	81
Philippians 2:5-8	84
Philippians 2:16-18	54
1 Thessalonians 5:21	125
2 Thessalonians 1:9	25
2 Thessalonians 3:13	127
1 Timothy 4:7-8	129
1 Timothy 4:12b-16	131

New Testament	Page
Titus 2:3-5	86,99
James 2:22	63
James 4:6-8	108
Hebrews 12:1-3	82,128
Hebrews 11:6	141
1 Peter 2:11	106
1 John 3:16-17	80
1 John 4:18	26
1 John 5:2-4	62

Index

101 Dalmatians, 112

A.K. (After Kids), 30

Abilities, 20, 23, 52, 70, 74

Abortion, 39

Accident, 16, 40

Agenda, 8, 75, 88, 119, 125

Anchor, 9, 41, 128

Animal heads, 97

Army, 51, 59

Ascension, 52

Authority, 109

Bag of tricks, 105, 106

Balance, 44, 117, 118

Barometer, 84

Battle cry, 11, 141

Battlefield, 9, 10

Beautiful, 13, 14, 19, 34, 41, 42, 43, 47, 49, 78, 137

Bedding, 33

Bedtime, 21

Bible, 2, 6, 7, 19, 25, 29, 31, 48, 59, 105, 106, 108, 115, 117, 119, 137, 138, 142

Birthday, 20, 78, 120, 130

Blaise, 5, 34

Boiling point, 45

Bold, 7

Bored, 89, 90, 110

Boundaries, 44, 84, 94, 124

Box, 33, 101

Boycott, 35, 36

Brea, 13, 16, 17, 50, 57, 58, 59

Breakfast, 115

Breaks, 106, 110

Bus, 35, 36

Busy at home, 86, 87, 99

Caged animal, 86

Calling, 5, 11, 59, 60, 61, 62, 67, 74, 75, 80, 81, 84, 86, 87, 90, 96, 122, 142

Career, 52, 62, 68, 69, 70, 77, 89

Carseat, 13, 21

Cause, 10, 19, 75, 134

Challenging, 7, 19, 63, 94, 109, 123

Cheerios, 120

Chores, 43

Christ, 8, 20, 24, 27, 48, 51, 54, 57, 79, 80, 81, 84, 101, 107, 108, 118, 122, 129, 130, 131, 132, 134, 142

Christmas, 17

Church plants, 52

Clay, 7, 46, 47

Coffee, 100

Commitment, 39, 60, 97

Community college, 34

Conference, 5, 6, 7, 8, 54

Confess, 9, 27, 120

Confession, 120

Controlling, 108

Convictions, 50

Crops, 32

Cross, 26, 27, 83, 84, 118, 128, 134

Crumbs, 33

C-section, 14, 49, 50, 51

Culture, 37, 41, 86

Darkness, 14, 111

Death, 17, 25, 26, 57, 84, 88

Deceived, 31, 94

Derail, 141

Diligence, 62, 131, 132

Disciples, 51, 52, 53, 61, 93, 99, 124

Discipline, 45, 93, 115

Disease, 25

Disobedience, 9

Distraction, 117

Distractions, 122, 126

Doctor, 13, 14, 15, 30, 49, 50

Dreams, 70, 76, 77, 79, 104

Drink offering, 54

Drip line, 93, 94

Earthquake, 137, 138

El Paso, 1, 2, 50, 97

Elliott, Elisabeth, 133

Email, 78, 124

Example, 60, 101, 131, 132

Exchange, 53, 54, 56, 57, 58

Exercise, 44

Expired dreams, 76

Extracurricular, 65

Extreme, 16, 60, 124

F5, 92

Facebook, 124

Faith, 17, 23, 51, 54, 57, 63, 65, 66, 77, 78, 79, 81, 90, 91, 92, 122, 128, 131, 132, 138, 141, 142

Family tree, 47, 48

Farm, 33, 78
Farmer, 32
Fashions, 44, 107, 120
Financial burden, 39
Flag, 9, 10
Focus, 24, 52, 84, 104, 107, 113, 115, 117, 120, 126, 129
Focus on the Family, 113
Follow me, 61, 118
Force, 10, 35, 40
Forgiveness, 20
Formulas, 23
Free will, 25, 26
Fruit, 58, 62, 77, 82, 87, 88, 125, 133
Frustration, 43, 45, 54, 63, 64, 105, 108, 114, 117, 118
Fun and fond memories, 43
Generation, 10, 51, 52, 59
Generous, 63, 64
Gift, 8, 23, 27, 37, 39, 40, 92, 120
Give us their hearts, 56
Glory, 8, 16, 17, 47, 48, 74, 83, 139, 142
Goals, 65, 76, 77, 89, 90, 96, 104, 113
Godless source, 9
Golden grain, 32, 33
Gospel, 57
Grace, 34, 41, 76, 78, 105, 106, 108, 114, 123, 132, 133, 134, 141
Grain, 32
Grandchildren, 33, 138
Great Commission, 52
Great project, 121, 122

Green, Keith, 131
Green, Melody, 131
Growth charts, 30
Guard your heart, 29
Gym, 105, 106
Harvest, 31, 32, 33
Healthy, 13, 16, 32, 51, 133
Hearers, 132
Heart energy, 129
Heart rate, 13
Heart that mothers sparingly, 63
Heart to mother generously, 63
Heartache, 15, 16, 48, 77
Heaven, 25, 29, 52, 57, 95, 96, 110
Heritage, 40, 47, 48, 49, 50, 51
Hissy fit, 7
Hobbies, 122, 125
Holocaust, 106
Homebodies, 87
Homework, 43
Hospital, 13, 14, 16, 17, 21, 22, 72, 103
Hunters, 97
Hymn writer, 102
Identity, 10, 67, 71, 72, 73, 74, 77, 78, 79, 80, 87, 116, 130
Impact, 55, 94, 95, 101, 102
Infinite Impact, 94
Influence, 10, 11, 30, 51, 88, 94, 101, 102
Interruption, 114, 120, 126
Investing, 31, 99, 101

Jesus, 24, 26, 27, 52, 57, 61, 80, 84, 107, 128, 129, 134
John, 61
Journey, 17, 19, 20, 23, 24, 29, 60, 61, 79, 81, 90, 140, 141
Juggling act, 43, 44
Keeping on, 103
Kernel, 58
Kiss, 33
Laundry, 43, 93, 114
Laying down my life, 19
Legos, 120
Letter, 48, 49
Life coach, 89, 90, 94
Life Magazine, 137
Living sacrifice, 62
Lonely, 59, 60
Losing them off the top, 33
Lost, 8, 15, 45, 48, 49, 51, 59, 68, 84, 126
Magazine, 9, 103
Majoring in the majors, 65
March on, my soul, 141
Marriage, 22, 23
Master's degree, 77, 85
Masterpiece, 17, 47, 56
Mature, 30, 32, 42, 107, 108
Meditating, 54, 101, 115
Memorization, 114, 123
Messy, 47, 64
Methodism, 102
Mirror, 87
Mission, 10, 51, 52, 90
Mistake, 40, 134

Mocked, 31

Models, 43, 46

Montgomery, Alabama, 35, 36

Mother in progress, 128

Mother in the Spirit, 88

Motherhood meeting, 104, 105

Mothering in the mini-van, 86

Movement, 10

Movies, 107

My little box, 101

Navigators, 54

Neediness, 21, 109

No regrets mothering, 65

Nobel, 68

Not taught, caught, 91

Nursing, 16, 17, 21, 72, 77

Nurturing, 47, 62

Oak tree, 42, 43

Obedience, 62, 80, 122, 134

Obstetrician, 50

Octopus, 44

Office Depot, 7

Old lady, 137, 138

Olympics, 83

Out-impact, 53

Pajamas, 34

Palace, 41, 42

Parks, Rosa, 34, 35, 36

Passion, 6, 8, 10, 60, 96

Patience, 20, 88

Peace, 57, 59, 88, 133, 137

Perseverance, 20, 82, 103, 134, 140

Perspective, 22, 23, 30, 40, 43, 50, 51, 53

Peter, 61

Phone, 44, 45, 89, 93, 94, 122, 124, 125

Picnic, 43, 44

Pillars, 41, 42, 43

Pit, 106

Plants, 41, 123, 124

Polly Pockets, 120

Position, 19, 54, 66, 69, 93, 108

Potential, 10, 11, 52, 68

Potter, 7, 46, 47

Power, 7, 92, 132, 136

Prayer, 16, 59, 133, 142

Precious moment, 23

Pregnant, 5, 38, 39

Prioritize, 63, 74

Psychologist, 9

Punishment, 26, 40

Puzzle, 71, 72, 73, 74

Quiet time, 114, 115, 116

Race, 32, 82, 83, 84

Reaping, 31

Refresh, 92, 105, 107, 109, 110

Regrets, 65, 79, 120

Relational, 25

Relationship with the Lord, 19, 107, 111, 117, 138

Restaurant, 37, 38, 89

Restlessness, 90, 109, 110

Restructuring, 79

Resurrection, 52

Reward, 40, 41, 42, 43, 95, 96, 97, 139, 142

Risks, 49, 50, 51, 142

Role models, 9

Roles, 79

Rolly, 112

Sacrifice, 5, 44, 53, 54, 55, 62, 80, 81, 82, 84, 121, 134

Santa Biblia, 137

Savior, 19, 24, 27, 47, 66, 80, 81, 142

Saying no, 119

Schedule, 96, 119, 124

School teacher, 8

Season, 29, 30, 31, 32, 33, 34, 53, 54, 98, 109, 124

Secrets, 24, 25, 26

Seed, 32, 58

Seek first, 71, 91

Segregation, 35, 36

Self-centered, 113

Shame, 24, 26, 27, 128, 140

Sharing the gospel, 53

Shelter, 42, 91, 137, 138

Shoes, 135, 136

Shopping, 7, 105

Siblings, 20

Silas, 138

Sin, 25, 26, 27

Skiing, 83

Skills, 20, 23, 52

Sleep, 14, 21, 22, 41, 75, 109, 123

Snowfall, 32

South Africa, 97

Sowing, 31, 32, 34, 63

Sparing, 63

Special breed, 87

Speech, 85, 96, 115, 131, 132

Speech Communication, 77

Spin, 103

Spirit, 6, 8, 48, 51, 88, 107, 116, 131, 132

Spiritual development, 65, 90

Spiritual work, 23

Sporadic, 139

Spring, 6, 32, 57, 111

Starbucks, 105, 106

Steam, 141

Steve, 5, 6, 14, 15, 21, 22, 33, 38, 49, 50, 54, 55, 56, 57, 65, 75, 79, 100, 104, 109, 113, 121, 122, 123, 125, 136

Storehouses, 116, 117

Storms, 42

Strength, 20, 24, 42, 47, 61, 88, 90, 108, 110, 134, 138, 140

Support system, 43

Tablets, 48

Talents, 20, 37, 67, 68, 74, 76, 80, 86

Taxidermy, 97

Ten Boom, Corrie, 106

Terrible two, 41

Teva, 137

Till, Emmett, 35

Top, 103

Tractor, 32

Transformation, 92

Treasure, 34, 37, 58, 95, 96, 97, 98

Tree, 48

Trials, 20, 31, 83, 140

Trinity, 25

Trotman, Dawson, 54

Trust, 59

Trustworthy, 9

Truth packs, 115, 116

Truth Project, 113

Turmoil, 19

TV, 9, 83, 107, 125

Umbilical cord, 13, 21

Unfulfilled, 110

University of Northern Colorado, 57

Van, 8, 86, 120

Veggie Tales, 103

Victim, 46

Victories, 20

Vision, 8, 29, 43, 66, 67, 86, 94, 110, 120

Wage, 25

Walks, 123

Waste, 45

Watchman, 108

Water, 55, 56, 120, 123

Wesley, Charles, 102

Wesley, John, 102

Wesley, Susanna, 102

What do you want to be, 68, 69

Wheat, 58

Wheel, 46, 47

Whole hearts, 50, 61, 62

Widow, 79

Wife, 79, 123, 131

Wisdom, 34, 57, 93, 100, 119, 120, 138, 139

Women relationships, 99

Women's Movement, 37

World, 5, 8, 9, 10, 11, 16, 17, 27, 34, 37, 40, 44, 48, 49, 51, 53, 59, 68, 69, 72, 76, 88, 92, 98, 101, 102, 103, 104, 105, 106, 107, 110, 113, 117, 118, 119, 122, 137

Worship, 62

Worthless idols, 105, 106

Wrestle, 19, 67, 81, 86, 95

Yield, 5, 126

Zeal, 8

Discussion Questions

These discussion questions are provided to help facilitate a small group of women going through the book together. Sometimes discussing what we are learning with others helps us build convictions instead of just superficially covering the material.

The best discussions tend to be when the discussion leader takes ownership of the topic and the questions. So feel free to add and subtract questions to develop a discussion time that meets the particular needs of your group.

Prologue – Positioning Yourself

From this week's readings, what were you most encouraged with? What did you read that was the most challenging?

How would you describe your current view of motherhood?

On a scale of 1-10, how much are you currently enjoying your motherhood journey? What has been the hardest part of motherhood for you so far?

From your experience, list the top two things that keep you going as a mother.

If your good friend was about to deliver her firstborn, what would you say to help prepare her for motherhood? What warnings would you give her?

What *did* you already know about motherhood that helped you in the early days of parenting? What do you *wish* you would have known about motherhood that you think would have helped you?

How would you describe your current relationship with Christ? In what way do you want it to grow? Give two descriptive words to help you articulate your answer.

Does a relationship with Christ *really* help in Motherhood? How? On a scale of 1-10, how much would you honestly say that your relationship with Christ currently helps you in your mothering?

What truth do you want to focus on until the group gets together again?

Have each person in the group share two things:

1. A prayer request that others can pray during this upcoming week.

2. An action step that they would like to apply this week.

Establishing Your Vision

From this week's readings, what were you most encouraged with? What did you read that was the most challenging? From the verses that were included, which one(s) did you most appreciate?

The Bible says that you reap what you sow. Does that encourage or discourage you? Why? Share examples in your life where that principle has proved to be true.

How hard would it have been for a whole community to boycott the bus system? How did they put up with the inconvenience? How does this story parallel motherhood?

Be honest. Do you *tend* to view children as gifts or burdens? How does your view affect your mothering? What circumstances have happened that tempt you to believe that children are burdens? Who in your life would you say exemplifies the belief that children are rewards? Why?

In your own words, describe the three different models of how mothering is often viewed.
- Every Day's a Picnic
- A Juggling Act
- A Frustration

What is the weakness of each view? How would you describe the "correct" view of motherhood? Get together with a partner and brainstorm a different analogy to describe God's view of motherhood. Share these other analogies with the group.

What did Kathleen mean when she wrote that an exchange of lives needs to occur in mothering? On a scale of 1-10, how difficult is it for you to "exchange" your life?

How does "falling to the ground and dying," fit into motherhood, and why is this necessary? What fears do you wrestle with when you think about giving up your life?

How would you describe God's calling on your life? How do you feel about it? In light of your calling, how do you want to start mothering differently?

What truth do you want to focus on until the group gets together again?

Have each person in the group share two things:
1. A prayer request that others can pray during this upcoming week.
2. An action point that they would like to apply this week.

Rebuilding Your Identity

From this week's readings, what were you most encouraged with? What did you read that was the most challenging? From the verses that were included, which one(s) did you most appreciate?

Describe God's calling on your life in as few words as possible. What part(s) of your description do you understand to be "correct", but you still have a hard time embracing? How does understanding your calling help you live without regrets?

Do you truly see motherhood as a noble calling, or is that just something that sounds nice in a book? Explain. How has your own view of the importance of mothering helped or hindered your mothering? Try to give specific examples.

What things are you inclined to find your worth and value from? How does that play out in your everyday life? According to the Bible, how should your true value be defined? What would look different in your life if correctly understood your true value?

Before you were a mother, what exciting dreams did you hold? What dreams were the hardest to give up? Why? How have your dreams changed as a mother?

What do you think Kathleen meant by "mothering in the minivan?" Is that really wrong? Why? What can you practically change to minimize "mothering in the minivan?"

How is the role of a coach similar to the role of a mother? How were you coached by your parents? In what areas do you wish you would have had more coaching? In what areas do your kids need coached? In your opinion, what are the three most critical areas to coach your children in? Why?

Describe the word "investment." How does it relate to mothering? How should a Christian mother manage her influence with her own children and her influence with other women?

We all have different spheres of influence. As a group, brainstorm what that list might include. In your opinion, does motherhood expand or narrow a woman's influence? Why?

What truth do you want to focus on until the group gets together again?

Have each person in the group share two things:
1. A prayer request that others can pray during this upcoming week.
2. An action step that they would like to apply this week.

Reinforcing Your Perseverance - Conclusion

From this week's readings, what were you most encouraged with? What did you read that was the most challenging? From the verses that were included, which one(s) did you most appreciate?

Do you feel like your mothering has been more influenced by God or by the world? How? Share two practical ways that a mother can minimize the world's influence. Which of the world's messages about motherhood do you think is most subtle? What of the world's messages about motherhood do you think is most damaging?

Be honest. What do you typically do to get refreshed and recharged? Is there anything wrong with that? If so, what?

Is it truly possible to be recharged by seeking God? What are some practical ideas on seeking God in the midst of mothering?

What is the difference between "eliminating" and "balancing?" When do you need to do one, and when do you need to do the other? Share examples of things that you have eliminated, and what the result has been in your life. Share examples of things you have balanced, and what the result has been in your life.

What boundaries in your life have helped you reach your goals as a mother? What boundaries would you like to add? What can you do to make your boundaries as effective as possible?

What does it mean to be a "mother in progress?" Did you grow up sensing that your parents were pursuing and growing in the Lord? How did that affect your relationship with them? Why is it important for our kids to see our weaknesses and struggles?

If a mother feels like there is something amiss between her and her child that she needs to be resolved, what would be healthy, biblically-based steps to go through that process? Is there anything that has happened between you and one of your children that the Lord is leading you to take steps to resolve?

Have each person in the group share two things:
1. A prayer request that others can pray during this upcoming year.
2. An action point that they would like to focus on for the next year of mothering.

Made in the USA
Charleston, SC
10 December 2011